The Yeshiva of the Telshe Alumni
Torah's Way Station in Riverdale

It is one of the oldest and, at the same time, one of the youngest institutions of higher Torah learning in the world. Established in the Riverdale community on the outskirts of New York City, a short distance from the major Jewish population centers of the New York metropolitan area, the Yeshiva of the Telshe Alumni is one of the youngest, most vibrant *yeshivos* in the world, with a venerable tradition going back over one hundred years.

The original Telshe Yeshiva was founded in 1875 in the small Lithuanian town of Telshe by Rabbi Eliezer Gordon. It was a time of great advances in Torah study brought on by the blossoming of the *yeshiva* movement, and within a short time, the Telshe Yeshiva took its place at the forefront of the great *yeshivos* of the period. Because of its rigid standards of academic excellence and the expert guidance and tutelage of its illustrious *roshei yeshiva*, many thousands of students from all over Europe, as well as a number of students from faraway America, flocked to the Telshe Yeshiva to develop as Torah scholars. After years of study, they would return to their native communities as leaders and exemplary figures, carrying the Telshe tradition to the far corners of the Jewish world.

In 1941, Nazi troops entered the town of Telshe and killed most of the faculty and student body in the *yeshiva*, but the small remnant that survived, under the leadership of Rabbi Eli Meir Bloch and Rabbi Chaim Mordechai Katz, reestablished the *yeshiva* with a handful of students in Cleveland, Ohio, in the fall of 1941. The new *yeshiva* became a rallying point for surviving students and alumni, and over the next two decades, the Telshe Yeshiva once again rose to world prominence as a prominent institution of higher Torah learning and one of the most important pioneers of the *yeshiva* movement in America.

Although countless students from the New York area attended

the Telshe *yeshivos* over the years, it was not until 1980 that the Yeshiva of the Telshe Alumni was established within the New York metropolitan area. The *yeshiva* is called the Yeshiva of the Telshe Alumni, because it was inspired and created by a founding committee of dedicated Telshe graduates who appreciated the importance of bringing the singular style and standards of Telshe scholarship to a wider public. After a brief stay in Westwood, New Jersey, the *yeshiva* relocated to a spacious, two-acre campus in Riverdale, New York, and its story is one of the great success stories of our times.

The Yeshiva of the Telshe Alumni has become one of the very finest institutions of its kind. The quality of the education is outstanding, rivalled only by the superb personal development engendered by the devoted faculty. As the *yeshiva* steadily grows in reputation and prestige, applications far exceed the capacity of the *yeshiva*, so that today the student body represents the flower of our Jewish youth, young men of exceptional talent and character who are being groomed to take their place among the leaders of the next generation. In the Yeshiva of the Telshe Alumni one can already catch a glimpse of the future of the Jewish people, and indeed, the future is bright.

Come see for yourself.

You'll be greeted and made welcome by the students. They'll bring you a chair, offer you a *siddur*, ask how they can help. You'll see a staff of profound, dedicated *Roshei Yeshiva* who represent the finest products of American and Israeli *yeshivos*. You'll see these educators guiding their students from early in the morning until late—very late—at night. You'll see classes that are not permitted to grow to a size that would inhibit this personal relationship. You'll see groups of physicians or professionals and business people from the community coming for their regular *shiur* in the Yeshiva. You'll see the cleanliness and order, and you'll feel the sense of mission that permeates the entire institution.

Seldom are expectations so well rewarded. That is why your much-needed suppport of YTA will accomplish so much.

RETURN TO THE
HEAVENLY CITY

Special Excerpt Edition

by
Menachem Gerlitz

CIS
P·U·B·L·I·S·H·E·R·S
New York · London · Jerusalem

Published and distributed
in the U.S., Canada and overseas by
C.I.S. Publishers and Distributors
180 Park Avenue, Lakewood, New Jersey 08701
(908) 905-3000 Fax: (908) 367-6666

Distributed in Israel by
C.I.S. International (Israel)
Rechov Mishkalov 18
Har Nof, Jerusalem
Tel: 02-538-935

Distributed in the U.K. and Europe by
C.I.S. International (U.K.)
89 Craven Park Road
London N15 6AH, England
Tel: 01-809-3723

Book and cover design: Deenee Cohen
Typography: Shami Reinman and Chaya Bleier

ISBN 1-56062-085-4

PRINTED IN THE UNITED STATES OF AMERICA

TABLE OF
CONTENTS

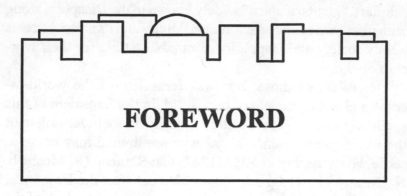

FOREWORD

"The heavenly Jerusalem corresponds directly to the earthly Jerusalem. In His great love of the earthly Jerusalem, He made another in the heavens."

(Midrash Tanchuma, Pekudey)

The holiness and uniqueness of Jerusalem did not diminish in the eyes of the Jewish people with the destruction of the Temple and the exile of the nation from their land. In fact, together with their yearning and prayers through the ages for the return of Israel to its land, the eyes of the people were constantly turned to every individual Jew or small group that succeeded in settling in Jerusalem; an aura of glory and holiness accompanied each one who went up to the mountain of G-d. Moreover, among these few individuals were righteous leaders and great scholars, "giants of spirit" widely known in the Diaspora, along with unknown saints who found in the city and its narrow streets a holy society and inspiration-a suitable setting for their worship of G-d.

Jerusalem of those days was Jerusalem of the world-to-come and not Jerusalem of this world. In the Jerusalem of this world whoever wishes to settle there may do so. In Jerusalem of the world-to-come only those who are invited may come to settle. From the day in 5027 (1267) that Ramban (R. Moshe b. Nachman) renewed the Jewish settlement after the long exile, there followed the steady immigration of individuals, and the influx of groups afterward—the first *chassidim*—the students of the Ba'al Shem Tov in the year 5537 (1777); the students of the Vilna Gaon in the year 5568 (1808); the students of the Chatham Sofer; and afterwards the various immigrations of the 5600s (nineteenth and twentieth centuries). All these were only the souls selected and invited to the holy city.

They left behind them the benefits of the Diaspora, rejecting all material goods believed necessary for existence, and came to this city to live a life of the soul, to develop in purity and holiness. Their daily lives were transformed into spirituality, from which we can learn the greatness and beauty of man in his ability to achieve wholeness in character and action. Yet together with this life style they also established, by selflessness and superhuman effort, the basis for the general renewal of Jewish settlement: Torah and welfare institutions, the first neighborhoods—in the beginning within the walled city close to the site of the Temple, and afterwards outside its walls.

The golden age of spirituality for this new Israel was the first half of the century beginning in 5600 (1840-1890). There was

6

hardly an observant writer of those times who did not lift his pen in praise of this renewal, in an attempt to describe the mortal-angels who walked about the holy city. Many non-Jewish writers too found in the Jerusalem of the day inspiration for their literary efforts.

There remains in Jerusalem even today a living miracle: the amazing mixture which came into being when every group that immigrated, each with its own characteristics and ideals, took the best from the other groups and created the well-known personality of the "*Yerushalmi*" Jew. Apart from the world-embracing wisdom and holiness which have become part of him, he is principally recognized by his humility—for he attributes none of this greatness to himself.

The holiness of the Temple site and of the City of Jerusalem emanates from the indwelling of the sacred spirit. This sacred spirit has never departed and never will leave the holy Temple site and the city. For it is stated, "And I shall desolate your sanctuaries," and from this our Sages learn that even though they are desolate they are called sanctuaries. So even today Jerusalem maintains its holiness.

[This excerpt, *Return to the Heavenly City*, features selections from the third and fifth volumes of *The Heavenly City* five-volume set (C.I.S. Publishers, Lakewood, New Jersey).]

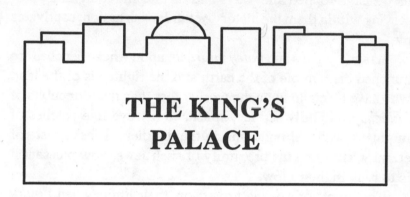

THE KING'S PALACE

A Letter With Heart

Enveloped in a veil of nobility, dressed in a mantle of antiquity—this is how Jerusalem appeared to the visitor of one hundred and fifty years ago. In a letter written by a Warsaw Jew who visited the city in that epoch, in 5584 (1824), which he despatched to his son in Poland, we find an outpouring of the soul and heart at the very sight of Jerusalem. This anonymous Jew, who was apparently gifted with poetic expression, wrote:

The chain of the Zion hills—Mounts Zion and Scopus and the Moabite hills—encircle the city like a setting for the diamond in a king's crown, like a superbly crafted protective fence for a carpet of roses.

Majestic rays of secrecy and mystery emanate from the cracks and clefts of its houses which overlap one another like flower petals. Even the sour odor of must, which wafts through its concave-topped alleyways and its ancient courtyards, preserving within them the history of the Jewish nation, captivates me.

Its synagogues and *batey midrash,* upon whose benches are hunched the humble of the earth and the righteous of the land who have no claim upon the world other than the four cubits of *halacha* and G-dly service, appear to my eye like patches of luminous white, shimmering in the darkness. I feel a taste of eternity, sitting in the proximity of such Jews; how pleasant it is to bask in their glow.

The founts of my heart overflow their limits when I mark these humbles of the earth emerging at daybreak from their immersion in the purity of the Shiloah waters, from the hidden depths of the cave of Rabbi Yishmael the High Priest, then on through the Dung Gate. Wrapped up in their caftans of gold stripe, the *peyoth* and beards which flow upon their clothing sparkling with spring water, and their faces generating light, they stride purposefully to perform their divine service, advancing from valley to hill, from hill to vale, wending their way among the pine trees sprung up from the rocks whose low branches sway in the soft mountain breeze.

Against the backdrop of the Holy City's beautiful, deep blue skies of dawn—at such hours when they are still misted with shredded white clouds between which peep the morning stars, revealing a horizon of mountain chains kissing the sky, when the cheeping of sparrow congregations and of chirping swallows flitting from roof to roof fills the atmosphere—one can almost sense the *Beith HaMikdash* as it was, firmly established upon its foundations; one can almost smell the aroma of incense wafting from the Holy of Holies. This was the very first time in my life that I wholly participated in the Song of Creation sung to a living G-d.

Even in the sustaining dew which falls at dawn, with which I had occasionally bathed my eyes, I feel the aura of souls which Rabbi Yehuda Halevi refers to in his famous lament.

My dear son, such is the view of the king's palace, without exaggeration. Surely it is worthwhile abandoning everything, liquidating all you own, to follow immediately on my heels.

Who Shall Climb The Mountain Of G-d?

We do not know if the son followed in his father's footsteps; neither do we know if the father himself succeeded in laying down roots in Jerusalem or returned to Warsaw.

The Jewish settlement in the Holy City was then meager in population, numbering only one hundred and twenty families in all. In disregard of the tribulations of *aliya* and indescribable hazardous adventure, they cast their souls to the winds and accepted the suffering of settling in Jerusalem, fulfilling in the fullest sense our Sages' expression that "Eretz Yisrael is acquired only through suffering."

Who, then, were these people who ascended the Mountain of G-d?

Oceans of tears have been shed throughout the generations over the prayer "*Ezkera Elokim*"—I recall, O *Hashem,* and sigh, when I see every city firmly established on its site whilst the city of G-d is downtrodden unto nether *Sheol*. For the rebuilding of the ruins of Jerusalem is the desire burning in the heart of every Jew, wherever he may be, since the time that the *tamid* sacrifice

11

was abolished and the Temple destroyed by the Roman emperor Adrian.

Throughout the generations, from the destruction of the *Beith HaMikdash* until the Arab takeover of Eretz Yisrael in the early 5250s, no Jewish foot trod in Jerusalem. In 5252 the Jews suffered a setback when they were banished from Spain where a settlement had existed from the time of the *churban*. But that year, which commences the decline of Spain, also dates the renascence of Jerusalem. Spanish Jews who made their way to Jerusalem through uncharted paths guarded the embers of Jerusalem lest these extinguish, and together with a tiny Ashkenazi congregation, which began to develop after the Rambam's *aliya* in that year, laid the foundation for the renewed settlement in Jerusalem. But in the ensuing years, only individual people joined it. The organized influx began only in later years, between 5537-5567 (1777-1807), with the advent of the disciples of the Ba'al Shem Tov and the Gra of Vilna, and later, the disciples of the Chatham Sofer. Most of the immigrants turned to the Galilean cities of Safed and Tiberias, but cores from these settlements were transplanted to the Jerusalem settlement so that it grew and flourished.

Groups among the elite of the nation knew that the settling of G-d's mountain, and the renewing of the community upon it had been their rabbis' dream, and they therefore sacrificed their material lives to this end.

The settlement began flourishing. The spiritual life within it reached a summit which could not be surpassed, but at the same time, the material situation grew increasingly worse. Housing owned by Jews was nonexistent. Apartments were rented from the Arabs within mixed courtyards, and the settlers were at their mercy, unprotected, abandoned, open to Arab pillaging and pogroms.

Thus Did They Suffer

The Arab-Turkish government, which then ruled the Middle East, was overrun with corruption and vice. Law and order were nonexistent in Jerusalem. The settlers were subjected to conditions of oppression and degradation from their Arab neighbors who lorded over them capriciously; there was no one who could uphold Jewish honor.

In addition, the original settlers suffered from a lack of minimal living conditions which did not disturb the Arabs, such as sewage and water supply. It was a common sight to see green pools of water in the city center which had stood thus for years breeding disease and plague. Thus, the city suffered terribly from the lack of water for drinking, bathing and laundry. Stored rain water from the rainy season was drawn from pits under the homes. When these were depleted, the Jews of the city were forced to purchase water at full price from the Arabs who lived in a village near the Silwan spring. The latter would transport water to the city in gourds or bloated goatskins, demanding an exorbitant price for this "golden" water.

All this was naught in comparison with the living conditions themselves. As the settlement grew, whole streets filled solely with Jewish dwellers, thus slowly forming the Jewish quarter within the city. Several streets were even given Jewish names while some wealthy Jews among the settlers succeeded in acquiring separate houses of their own. The Jewish settlement, however, was limited and concentrated within the city walls.

Outside the walls lay desolation, wasteland and impregnable boulders.

Inside, the crowding was unbearable, and the Arab landlords took advantage of this fact with full wiliness. From week to week they raised the rents, lording it over the Jewish population. The tenants were forced to pay rather than be evicted together with their families and possessions and thrown into the streets in the middle of the night.

It was during these mad days that the Jews of Jerusalem began dreaming of breaking through the walls which confined them and going forth to the expanse outside to establish a new city of spacious houses, beyond the walls.

The first awakening to this concept took place, actually, in 5587 (1827), during the first visit to the famous English Jewish philanthropist, Sir Moses Montefiore, but the real practical application began only in 5607 (1847) with the organized effort to establish the first Jerusalem *shchuna*.

The first neighborhood was established within the city gates. Batey Machseh, near Mount Zion, was established by the heads of Pakum, an organization founded by Rabbi Zvi Hirsh Lerin and his munificent son, Rabbi Akiva, which was Amsterdam-based and aimed at establishing a settlement in Eretz Yisroel. It was financed by the donations of the leading personalities of those times, Rav Yakov Ettlinger, author of *Aroch Laner*; Rabbi Shamshon Rafael Hirsch from Frankfurt and the Rothschild family. Success shone upon this *shchuna*, and it became more firmly established from year to year, eventually becoming one of the symbols of the city and the dwelling place of many great figures until its destruction in 5708.

The second neighborhood, built outside the walls, though right near by, was called Mishkenot Sha'ananim or Yemin Moshe. It was funded from the estate of the philanthropist Judah Touro from New Orleans, under the trusteeship of Sir Moses Montefiore, who increased the building fund many times over.

Construction of the two sections was under way by 5615-17 (1855-57). Montefiore also established a hospital in Mishkenot Sha'ananim, as well as a weaving factory and a windmill for grinding flour to provide a livelihood for the settlers. But while Batey Machseh grew and flourished without any means of support for its settlers, Mishkenot Sha'ananim was not graced with similar success. Montefiore himself visited Jerusalem three more times with the prime purpose of developing the neighborhood: right after completion of construction in 5617 (1857), later in 5626 (1866) and again in 5636 (1876), paying out considerable sums to many Jerusalem Jews aside from the monthly stipend, to assure their settling this section.

During his visit in 5626 (1866), Montefiore even found a solution to the problem of wild animals that roamed through the section at night. He hired a Jerusalem blacksmith, Reb Eliyahu Zalman Bassan to contrive a huge iron trap. This trap was centrally located and baited with roasted meat. Each night it lured and trapped various predatory animals which were then transferred to zoos abroad.

Nevertheless, all of these measures did not succeed in transferring all Jews of Jerusalem to the other side of the city walls.

The seething closeness erupted when a decimating plague broke out in 5626 (1866), felling in its wake many great Jerusalem figures. Reb Binyamin Rotzigel, an honest and worthy doctor, who labored devotedly to save the city, was also struck down. His tombstone bore the following inscription:

> An honest and simple man
> A doctor who protected the entire city
> Sanctifying his body
> In particular when the measure of justice
> was being visited upon our Holy City

At this same time, a plague was also wreaking havoc in Transjordan. Throngs of refugees flocked to Jerusalem and the congestion was suffocating.

During this period, other sections and buildings were also built, both within the city walls and outside it, nearby. One small *shchuna*, built between Damascus Gate and the Lion Gate, was called Baba Cheta or Wheat Gate. Others were the Kirya Ne'emana section of Nissen Beck near Damascus Gate and Machane Yisrael, which was built by the rabbi of the Mugrabi congregation, Rabbi David ben Shimon (Dvash), but these hardly made a dent in the pressure felt throughout the city.

The Resolution Of Priority

In 5617 (1857), a group of the city's powerful leaders met to deal with the stifling problem of housing, founding an organization called Bonei Yerushalayim (Builders of Jerusalem). It was headed by the cream of the city's population: Rabbi Yoshe (Yosef) Rivlin and Rav Eliezer Dan Ralbag, both of them son in laws of Rav Yosef Schwartz, author of *Tvuoth Ha'aretz*;

Rabbi Avraham Brisker; Rav Yeshaya Orenstein, son-in-law of Rabbi Moshe Maggid; Rabbi Arye Leib Horowitz, son-in-law of Rabbi Eliyahu Yosef Rivlin; Reb Zalman Baharan; Rabbi Zalman Baharil Levi and Rabbi Ben Zion Leon.

These lions guaranteed the realization of the settlement venture but the eternal problem was budging the Jerusalem population from its place. After much discussion and consultation, they reached the conclusion that the initiative for building must originate from the Jews of the city itself who would know how to adapt the prospective community to their needs, rather than from outside, from the generosity of philanthropists abroad. Meanwhile, something had to be done to ease the problem within the city itself. The organization turned to the leaders of the city and instituted the Resolution of Priority.

This resolution stated: "Every Jew renting an apartment from a non-Jew acquires priority or claim to this apartment, and until he leaves it of his own free will, no other Jew is permitted to rent the same apartment."

The right of claim, transmitted from father to son, was worth a great deal in those years. The right of claim held a prestigious position in a family's assets and provided a measure of respite from the caprice of Arab landlords.

This resolution was good, however, only as long as the Arab landlords did not unite, while they still managed their affairs separately without coordination. By miracle, the right of claim resolution served Jerusalem Jewry for a long period and protected them. However, the *askanim* were constantly fearful lest the Arab landlords unite in raising the rentals. They knew that if that ever happened, they would be forced to capitulate and pay whatever price was demanded if they did not wish to renew the

17

sad spectacle of people sleeping on the city streets. Eventually their fear became reality.

Nashishivi Raises The Rent

At that time, a new leader rose to power from among the Arab ranks, Nashishivi by name. Boasting fabulous wealth, including numerous houses, Nashishivi was related to many of the city's landlords and made a practice of representing illiterate landlords in court. When all was said and done, he held the keys to most of the dwellings in the Old City.

Aside from his vast power, Nashishivi was wily and cunning, knowing how to utilize his power and exploit the helplessness of the Jewish population. One day he decided to do exactly that.

Shortly before the month of Muchram—the expiration and renewal date set by Moslems for rental contracts—Nashishivi took all the keys to the apartments and refused to negotiate with Jews who already held rental claims. He approached the representative of the Jewish community, the president of the Bonei Yerushalayim organization, Rabbi Yoshe Rivlin, to negotiate a general rental raise, warning that if his demand was not met, no landlord would renew a contract and the tenants would all be evicted. To the amazement of Jerusalem Jewry, Rabbi Yoshe refused to discuss the matter with the aggressive Arab. Nashishivi proudly boasted that he would yet break him. Jerusalem Jewry stood by on the sidelines, awaiting further developments.

Perhaps if Nashishivi had approached every tenant individually, they may have capitulated, each one fearing for his own skin, but his arrogance in challenging the head *askan* brought about his own downfall.

Two weeks before Muchram, Nashishivi sent a warning to Rabbi Yoshe Rivlin with an ultimatum of two weeks, at the end of which rentals would be doubled.

The Arab messenger reached Rabbi Yoshe's home. The latter guessed the purpose of his visit and without even opening the door, called from the window curtly and decisively.

"Tell the one who sent you that I promise him that by Muchram, rents will be halved!"

Nashishivi was stunned by this reply. He had certainly expected a round of negotiations and stiff bargaining but such Jewish arrogance was beyond belief. Who knew the housing situation better than he, after all? The majority of Jewish inhabitants lived in Arab houses. Where would they all find other housing in such a short period?

On the other hand, Nashishivi was well acquainted with Rabbi Yoshe's stature and knew full well that he had the power to back his words. Rabbi Yoshe was not one to shower wild, unsubstantiated threats. But how? From where? He could not imagine.

Nashishivi weighed the matter carefully. What was more precious to him, his pride or his money? He cast his vote for the latter. Arranging his garish red *kafiya* on his head, a symbol of importance, he took himself to Rabbi Yoshe's home.

"And what does the Jewish *Chacham* expect to do?" he challenged, hugging his round paunch importantly. "Where do you expect to house the Jewish population once they are evicted?"

"Never fear," replied Rabbi Yoshe, "we will care for them.

They will not have to sleep on the street."

"Do you expect to gather them in the Churvath Rabbi Yehuda HeChassid courtyard? Even if you were to crowd all the Jews in the city side by side after a fast day, the place would not contain them."

"I have already told you," replied Rabbi Yoshe, "that I will take care of our Jews. They will not have to fast or be herded together. The Churva courtyard is not my solution."

"Then we will meet again on the coming Muchram," the Arab boiled, slamming the door behind him.

"I am certain that by then you will cut your rentals by half," Rabbi Yoshe calmly repeated to Nashishivi's retreating back.

That very evening, Rabbi Yoshe gathered the members of the Bonei Yerushalayim organization to plan in detail what they had long discussed, the establishment of the Nachlath Shiva neighborhood. Seven members signed an agreement to settle there as soon as it was established. The first three signatures were those of Rabbi Yosef Rivlin, Rabbi Yoel Moshe Salomon, who later founded Petach Tikva, and Reb Binyamin Beinish Salant, son of the city's chief rabbi, Rav Shmuel Salant.

On Muchram of that year, Nashishivi truly did halve his rents, together with the other Arab landlords. Fear of the Jews suddenly descended upon them, compounded by the threat of new housing, for they realized that their insistence upon inflated rents would only prod more and more Jews to leave the city.

Rabbi Yoshe's Mentor

The above-mentioned Rabbi Yoshe Rivlin was really the

second Rabbi Yoshe. He was preceded by his cousin, the first Rabbi Yoshe Rivlin, who was similarly one of the chief *askanim* in Jerusalem.

The first Rabbi Yoshe was not as famous as his cousin, but not because he was less worthy or because he was confined to his four cubits of Torah study. On the contrary, from his early youth he dedicated himself wholly to serving the public and the individual need. He was not as well known, however, because he died young. When the epidemic of 5626 (1866) broke out in Jerusalem, he was one of its first victims. Nonetheless, the people of Jerusalem had had their chance to acquaint themselves with him and the great personalities of the city respected him for his good deeds and successful undertakings.

The first Rabbi Yoshe was also a trustee of Kolel Vilna, which numbered most of the Ashkenazi community among its members. Iron safes were as yet unknown in Jerusalem and the trustee served also as guardian of the cashbox which consisted of a large cloth pouch, hung from his neck by a drawstring and worn between his chest and shirt. Stipend monies arrived from Lithuania from time to time, and when they did, Rabbi Yoshe himself would make the rounds of the stipend recipients to assure immediate delivery of these funds. If he happened to meet one of the "customers" who appeared on the *kolel* list on the city street, he would not hesitate in the least or feel ashamed, but would seat himself upon a stone fence or stoop and trace the man's name as it appeared on the list, together with his vital statistics of family status and the sum which the *gabbaim* had allotted him. There were several factors which determined this sum—personal status, dependents, etc. After these introductory remarks by which he tried to convince the recipient that the sum had not been determined by caprice or personal preference, Rabbi Yoshe would remove his pouch and count out the money that was coming to that man, along with his personal blessing and good wishes.

This was Rabbi Yoshe's lifelong preoccupation—making the rounds of his beneficiaries' homes, as they appeared on his long list and dispensing their just stipends. Finding each and every one was no simple matter, but Rabbi Yoshe spared no effort. On the same day that the money arrived, he would trudge through sleet and snow, visiting the same person several times if need be, until he found him at home. Why? Because he was a faithful public servant who intimately knew the poverty his families suffered and the hopes they pinned on this stipend. Retaining these funds overnight constituted to him a specific prohibition of "*talin*"—withholding the debtor's vital vessel (whether clothing, tool, etc.) overnight, knowing well enough that lives might even be at stake, as the Torah states, "For he is withholding life."

After a backbreaking day of continual trudging, he would return to his humble, poorly lit home to eat supper by the light of a flickering oil lamp.

What did Rabbi Yoshe's supper consist of? A handful of dried figs which he had purchased along the way. He would first inspect them by the lamplight to see if they were wormy. Those suitable for consumption would be spread upon a piece of dark bread. This was his entire supper.

Tired, weary, neither hungry nor yet sated, Rabbi Yoshe would take his *Gemara* in hand and complete his daily *shi'ur*. He would then recite the *Shema*, lay his head on his hand and thus fall asleep. Neither pillow, featherbed or arranged bed were his lot, only the table as a leaning post for his hand and his hand as a pillow for his head. He would nap thus until midnight. Then he would rise like a lion, full of energy, and stride purposefully to the *beith midrash* where he learnt until dawn, the time for his *vathikin* prayers. He would then rise, his prayers coinciding with sunrise, to continue on with renewed public service and lighten the suffering of the Jerusalem population.

Deeds of the fathers were signposts for the cousin, the second Rabbi Yoshe, who learned from his predecessor to emulate such devotion and concern for Jerusalem Jewry.

A Condition in the *Tenaim*

The second Rabbi Yoshe, rebuilder of Jerusalem's ruins, with whom we are now concerned, already stood out in his childhood as one who was gifted with unique talents. When he was only fourteen, he was acknowledged to be one of the most brilliant young minds of the Etz Chayim *yeshiva*. A genius, he wove all sorts of plans for improving and advancing the quality of life for Jerusalem Jewry.

In 5615 (1855), when Sir Moses Montefiore visited Jerusalem and Rabbi Yoshe was a mere eighteen years old, he volunteered to help set up the new neighborhood outside the wall. This offer pleased the lord who invited Rabbi Yoshe to London to make his program workable. One of the people present at one of these meetings suggested that Montefiore himself settle in Jerusalem but young Yoshe vetoed it. "The program can be actualized only if Sir Moses remains in London and I in Jerusalem."

That very year, he became engaged to a young girl from the Goldschmidt family. Just before the *tenaim* was read aloud, Yoshe turned to the bride's brother, Reb Moshe Yitzchak Goldschmidt, saying,

"Since the *tenaim* call for a commitment on both sides 'not to conceal anything from one another,' I must confess that I myself plan to settle and to convince others to settle with me outside the walls in a Jewish settlement which I will found."

Hearing this, the *mechutan* wished immediately to cancel the engagement, for in the view of those times, such thoughts pointed to an unstable, unbalanced young man with suicidal intentions, but his friends and relatives deterred him from doing so, arguing that such an idea would never be more than a pipe dream.

Rabbi Yoshe never stopped dwelling on this plan, however, verbally and in action. He was always finding signs and portents that the present was a suitable time to expand the settlement in Jerusalem, substantiating his claim with quotes from *Midrashim*, *Ketuvim* and any other holy written source, while his listeners would nod their heads knowingly and murmur, "It is his monomania."

When his relatives in the Diaspora learned of Rabbi Yoshe's programs, they invited him to come and discuss this idea firsthand, thinking that he would retract his words himself.

His power of persuasion was so great, however, that they joined his way of thinking and were even able to secure through pressure a substantial sum which they put at his disposal to carry out his plan. This money served Rabbi Yoshe as a base for acquiring land. It was soon evident that he was being aided by Heaven in his efforts.

24

He made various attempts at acquiring land during the next ten years, but the sale was never consummated for some reason or other. He finally did succeed, however, in 5627 (1867).

On the fourth of Iyar, 5629 (1869), the first assembly of the Nachlath Shiva settlers took place, and on Lag B'omer of that year, the cornerstone of the first house was laid.

The Trials Of The First Settlers

Eretz Yisrael is acquired through suffering; Jerusalem is acquired through supreme suffering.

It is customary for a person buying any object to regret the money he has to pay but to rejoice with his purchase. In buying land in the Jerusalem of yore, the purchaser suffered at both ends. To begin with, the settlers had to pay dearly without even acquiring the land. While the money was still jingling in the seller's pocket, there suddenly materialized another claimant to that very site, document in hand to prove that he was a partial landowner through partnership or as the sole owner.

How could that be? The Turkish government had its own solutions.

Neither money nor suffering alone could buy property. In addition, one needed a large measure of intelligence to counter Arab duplicity. Buyers would usually work on convincing prospective sellers that they were buying land to plant wheat for *shmura matza* and not for housing, otherwise there would be no sale, since the Arabs feared losing their source of ready income through rentals within the Old City. Most landowners were also the landlords of the apartments in the Jerusalem courtyards and begrudged any easing of their extortionary grip on the housing market. Nevertheless, despite the true need for farming land for wheat, Arab suspicions increased from day to day and Jewish *askanim* were forced to resort to various tricks.

The first acquisition of land for Nachlath Shiva was done by and on the name of Alta, the wife of Rabbi Arye Leib Horowitz, who appeared in the land office of the Turkish authorities heavily veiled and in Arab dress. Somehow she succeeded in allaying the fears of both sellers and government clerks, who despised the Jews equally.

The lot bought by the members of Bonei Yerushalayim was a costly one in both suffering and money. No wonder, then, that the families, who endured much, often poured their wrath upon Rabbi Yoshe to the extent of even marking the door of his home with a bold inscription which read, "Rabbi Yoshe endangers lives." But Rabbi Yoshe, who was firm in his belief and the justification of his ends, paid no attention, especially when he saw the distinctive hand of G-d assisting him in his endeavors.

Rabbi Chaim Mann, the Jerusalem genius, used to tell over that whenever Rabbi Yoshe needed to apply to the authorities for their good will or to abolish difficult decrees for the welfare of the Jewish settlement, he would rise early that day and recite the complete *Tehillim* fervently and with copious tears. Only then would he go before the authorities. Is it a wonder, then, that his prayers were answered and his purpose accomplished?

Overnight Lodging in Nachlath Shiva

All of the Jerusalem community participated in the cornerstone laying ceremony which took place on Lag B'omer—the

26

settling families, to be sure, and the rest, to share in the joyous occasion of the expansion of Jerusalem. Most came, however, to inspect the site that Rabbi Yoshe had chosen to found his "village" and to witness the marvel of the realization of his plans.

Within a mere two months, the first houses were already completed, ready to receive their inhabitants. Actually, only Rabbi Yoshe himself dared spend the night in his home outside the walls, amidst the desolate wasteland. Even his family refused to join him, remaining within the walls at night. Every evening, he would leave for Nachlath Shiva, accompanied by Rabbi Nissim Shamash, and every morning his family and friends would wait to see if the miracle had again happened and he had survived the night.

As a special *segula* protection, Rabbi Yoshe began writing a *Seifer Torah* in his new home and the merit of his undertaking did indeed stand him in good stead. He had been married for fifteen years without any issue, but lo! After living only one year in his new home, dating from the time he began writing the verse, "And he begot sons and daughters." Jerusalem rejoiced in the news that a daughter had been born to his wife. She was duly named Nechama, a comfort.

The rest of the settlers were temporary visitors in their new homes, for the fear imposed on them by the wilderness overcame their strong desire to settle. In order to crush this fear, Rabbi Yoshe would often invite visitors and detain them until nighttime when they were forced to remain overnight outside the protection of the Jerusalem walls. But the sense of terror could not be overcome too easily. One time, one of the seven original settlers, who was truly a brave man, accepted Rabbi

Yoshe's invitation to visit and remain overnight. In the middle of the night, however, he suddenly awoke in panic and, gathering all of his bedclothes, ran to hide under Rabbi Yoshe's bed for the rest of the night. Another guest of Rabbi Yoshe's refused to forgive his host for detaining him. When he awoke the following morning, he refused to taste a morsel, claiming that he must first hurry home to say the *Hagomel* blessing in gratitude for having survived the night!

His friends once begged him on an Arab holy day to forgo that one night of sleeping outside the walls, from actual fear for Rabbi Yoshe's life. When they saw that they could not persuade him, they detained him forcibly in his brother's house within the walls. Rabbi Yoshe outsmarted them, however, by escaping through the window, claiming that if he missed even one night, people might interpret it to mean that the place was truly unsafe. The entire project would then be worthless.

Rabbi Yoshe once had to travel to Jaffa for several days. His friends decided to seize this opportunity and, as soon as he left his home, hired workers to dismantle the windows and doors. This, they thought, would force him to abandon his *"meshugas"* of sleeping alone in the house, for he would surely conclude this to be the work of vandals, proof that the place was truly unsafe. Rabbi Yoshe had just left the city, however, when he suddenly recalled something important that he had forgotten, an item that he required for his trip. Returning home, he surprised the "vandals" at their job. His friends were now convinced that Providence was assisting him to drive a durable stake in the construction of Jerusalem and left him alone.

Neither was Rabbi Yoshe deterred when he was forced to sacrifice of his very blood in the establishment of the *shchuna*.

His wife, Sara Zipa, was once hanging out her laundry by the gate of the house. Suddenly an Arab bandit attacked her, his knife drawn. Sara Zipa did not lose her wits. Exhibiting tremendous bravery, she knocked the weapon from his hand and stabbed him with it. The Arab fell to the ground in a pool of blood. After this struggle, however, she suffered a stroke and died in the prime of life.

Her young daughter, Nechama, contracted cholera from the swamps near Nachlath Shiva and died within a few days, at the age of four.

After these heavy blows, which followed shortly upon each other, Jerusalem Jewry assumed that Rabbi Yoshe would abandon his plans and return to the security of the walls. Rabbi Yoshe, however, saw these tragedies as the true acquisition of Eretz Yisrael. After such sacrifices he was certain that the city could be conquered. With renewed effort and increased energy, he set about expanding the settlement outside the walls, and indeed, from that time on, he succeeded. From then on, he found a more willing ear among people for his project. Slowly but surely, the families began inhabiting their new homes.

To the amazement of Jerusalem Jewry, at this very time, Rabbi Yoshe withdrew from his work in the *shchuna* in order to spin some new plans, this time for the larger settlement, known as Meah Shearim.

White Stones

What particular problem caused Rabbi Yoshe to withdraw from Nachlath Shiva?

With every benefit that a person enjoys, there are stings which *Hakadosh Baruch Hu* sends to test His creations. So, too, was the case with the settlement outside the walls. The Jews of the Old City were an obstinate lot when it came to matters of religion, due to the influence of the Jerusalem rabbis who, throughout the years, stood on guard lest anyone "capture the queen from within" and allow G-dless infiltrators a foothold inside the Holy City.

Yet, when slowly but surely the Nachlath Shiva community began to stand on its feet, to the joy of every Jew within the city, the dreaded break appeared.

At that time, enlightened emissaries were sent from abroad to convince Jerusalem Jewry to send their children to the first secular school, Lemel, which was founded in 5616 (1856). Despite promises of all sorts of benefits, the representatives did not succeed in wooing more than five students altogether, four Sefardic youths and one Ashkenazi, who was none other than the son of the Nachlath Shiva resident, Yehoshua Yellin.

Jerusalem rabbis were embittered over his breach. Could it be that one from their own camp, from their very walls, should dare to batter at the wall of Orthodox Jewry? In addition to the *cherem* prohibition which Jerusalem rabbis had long since declared against the school itself, they now decreed Yehoshua Yellin's excommunication, cutting off his monthly *kolel* stipend as well.

Yehoshua Yellin did not let the matter stand at that. He fought this measure fiercely, even going abroad to solicit the intervention of Jewish leaders on his behalf to remove the *cherem* and reinstate him on the *kolel* list, but no one was willing to interfere in the holy battle of Jerusalem Jewry against secularism. Indeed, the poison of this school worked upon the boy for the rest of his life for David Yellin later became one of the chief leaders of secular Zionism, persecuting Orthodox Jewry in Jerusalem with a vengeance.

This, then, was the reason behind the defection of Rabbi Yoshe Rivlin and several other G-d fearing settlers from the company of these seditionists and the settlement of Nachlath Shiva.

Many saw in this a Heavenly punishment for the settlement, which did not have the blessings of the Orthodox leadership at its outset. Indeed, over the years there were only a few religious settlers in Nachlath Shiva, and the settlement was eventually pushed into an insignificant corner.

Rabbi Yehoshua Weisman, who survived past the age of one hundred emigrating from Germany in the latter part of his life, wrote:

"In my childhood, my parents, who were of German descent, lived in the new settlement of Nachlath Shiva. In 5642, a terrible epidemic broke out in the *shchuna*. At first my father of blessed memory, who was the *shamash* of the *shul*, passed away, to be followed shortly after by my mother. I was left an abandoned orphan. When this became known to my family in Germany, my mother's brother arrived to take me back with him. He arrived in the week of Succoth and was scheduled to return right after the *yom tov*. During the holiday, we both made the rounds of the city's leaders but on Simchat Torah my uncle decided to take me to *daven* in the Batey Machseh *shul* in the Old City, by Rav Yosef Chayim Sonnenfeld, having heard so much about his manner of celebrating Simchat Torah and his dancing during *hakafoth*.

"Throughout his life, even in advanced age, when he wore the crown of Jerusalem's rabbinate, Rav Yosef Chayim would gather the children in the *beith midrash* on Simchat Torah and dance with them for hours on end to *Ein Keilokeinu* sung in Yiddish as solo and chorus.

"I also joined the circle of children. Rav Yosef Chayim, who had known my parents and family and was aware that I had been orphaned, befriended me. He took his place in the circle next to me, stretched out his pure hand to me and led me in dance. Suddenly he stopped the circle of dancing children. The adults continued dancing with the *Sifrei Torah*, but he turned to me, saying, 'Yehoshua'le, how do you explain our singing and exclaiming that, "There is no G-d like our G-d"? and then asking, "who is like our G-d"? Is it not like a question after the answer?'

"I was moved almost to tears by this question. What did the *rav* want from me, a little fellow, and an orphan to boot? Why did he turn to me, I wondered, innocently thinking that perhaps he had seen something written on my forehead, perhaps some sign of guilt on my face. I was thoroughly ashamed.

"Rav Yosef Chayim touched my cheeks with his pure hands and soothed me. 'I did not direct the question to you in particular, sweet child. It did not occur to me that you must provide the right answer to all the children; you just happened to be right nearby.'

"The *rav* looked at me with his intelligent, calming gaze, and began his explanation, all the children crowding around to listen.

surely know, my child, that there are explorers who ll kinds of treasures and antiquities in caves. These caves are sometimes long, dark and winding. Once inside, it is difficult to find the way with smooth, white stones so that when they have finished their exploration, they will be able to return.

" 'Know, my son, that this world is like such a long, dark and winding cave. The person inside is like the explorer, always seeking and searching. Sometimes he penetrates too deeply and all kind of question arise—How? Why? Wherefore? Which way out? He may even begin questioning "Who is our G-d?" and come to total rejection. There is a safeguard against this, however, and that is to return the very same way that one entered.

" 'When we first declare that there is no G-d like ours and no Lord like ours, then even if we find ourselves in deep waters or chasms, we will not lose our way. These are *Klal Yisrael's* white stones,' Rav Yosef Chayim concluded with emotion and again formed a circle with the children and resumed the dancing with renewed fervor.

"Rav Yosef Chayim sensed the evil winds flowing through the Nachlath Shiva section, the winds of the atheism which was still in its infancy in the Holy City. He warned the young orphan child against it before the boy's departure to the Diaspora, lest he be tainted by it in any degree."

In his last days, Rabbi Yehoshua would recurrently refer to this story, adding with a sigh,

"I have experienced much during my long sojourn on earth and suffered many tests from the time I was brought to Germany. I lived through two world wars, staying in detention camps and concentration camps. I lost my entire family—wife, sons and daughter. I almost despaired of all hope but when I recalled Rav Yosef Chayim's words and the white stones of the

33

Jerusalem *tzaddik* whom I had been fortunate to know in my childhood, I saw them—and still see them to this very day—as rays of light in the great darkness.

"This world is not ours. It has a Leader Who knows how to answer all the questions and philosophical queries that exist," Rabbi Yehoshua would conclude.

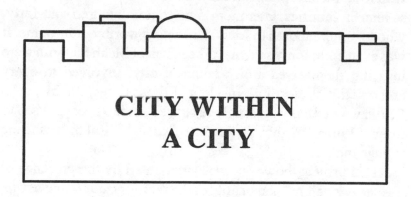

CITY WITHIN
A CITY

The Founding of Meah Shearim

When an elite group of Jerusalem Jews began weaving their dream of establishing the *shchuna* of Meah Shearim, they were not considered pioneers, having been preceded by the settlers of Mishkenot Sha'ananim in 5620 (1860), Machane Yisrael in 5628 (1868) and Nachlath Shiva in 5629 (1869).

Nevertheless, Meah Shearim, planned and executed under the guidance of the city's leaders, differed in character and purpose. It was not a mirror of the first *shchunoth* founded by individual philanthropists, nor a copy of Nachlath Shiva, for although in the latter, the original settlers themselves designed the neighborhood and shouldered the responsibility for it, they were too few in number to impose a stamp of individuality upon their *shchuna*.

In contrast, Meah Shearim encompassed a large public

which at its inception already numbered one-hundred-and-seventeen families, later increasing to one-hundred-and-forty, who together labored to found a *shchuna* worthy of its name. It was even commonly said that the settlers of Meah Shearim were building themselves a city within a city. Involved in every construction project in Jerusalem of those times, Rabbi Yoshe Rivlin was actively present here as well. In fact, people used to refer to him as "Rabbi Yoshe *Shtetlmacher*", Rabbi Yoshe the village maker.

This project, however, was augmented by the presence of the "heavyweight" personality of the famous *tzaddik* and *askan*, Reb Zalman Levi, or as he was commonly known, Reb Zalman Baharan (ben HaRav Nachum). It is worthwhile, at this point, to mention his great father, the saintly Rav Nachum of Shadik, one of the brilliant minds of the Old City. Reb Zalman threw himself wholeheartedly into the founding and establishment of the *shchuna*. What Rabbi Yoshe was to Nachlath Shiva, Reb Zalman was to Meah Shearim.

The time was Cheshvan, 5634 (1873). The *yishuv* within the walls was bursting at the seams. A new wave of immigration added to the terrible crowding which had existed previously, and which, coupled with the lack of minimal sanitary conditions, made housing conditions intolerable. The suffering was indescribable.

It has been said that "no one ever complained that there was no room to lodge in Jerusalem." When did this hold true? When there was no one to restrict place. But when the landlords constricted and confined the facilities of people wishing to lodge in the city, it was a different matter. This situation prepared the ground—it tempered the souls of Jerusalemites who had secretly hoped for something like this—for the man who would come and compel them to burst through the wall and settle outside it.

Reb Zalman Baharan felt, with his acute instincts, that the situation was ripe for this realization of the dreams of the city's population, and he therefore called a general assembly to discuss the problem.

The Meah Shearim Corporation was established on *Rosh Chodesh Kislev*, 5634 (1873), taking its name from a phrase found in the weekly portion of that particular week, *Toldoth*. The future settlement was supposed to have been named Rechovoth, which is also mentioned in the *parsha*, "And he called its name Rechovoth, saying, 'Now G-d has expanded us and we will be fruitful in the land.'" In the course of time, however, the name Rechovoth fell into disuse and the *shchuna* assumed the name of the corporation, Meah Shearim, a name which it bears to this very day.

How amazing it is to note the great love these people bore to the remnant of our beloved *Beith Hamikdash*, to have wished so fervently to live in its proximity at all times.

The corporation considered two sites—the one upon which Meah Shearim was eventually built and the plot known today as the Russian Compound which lay closer to the main thoroughfare.

The first was desolate wasteland, full of snakes and scorpions. Residents of the *shchuna* used to say that "since the time of the *churban*, probably no one stepped foot there." But while the second site was closer to the highway, the first had the advantage of being closer to the Wailing Wall, remnant of the Holy Temple, and therefore closer to the hearts of the settlers. Had it not been for dread of the many dangers abounding there, they would not have hesitated in the least in preferring this site.

They brought the dilemma before the famous Rav Meir Auerbach, author of *Imrei Bina* and head of the Jerusalem rabbis. The great man ruled as follows, quoting the Torah, "'If the place which *Hashem* your G-d has chosen to rest His Name is too distant,' meaning, if the place is far, it is so because you have made it so. This is a clear indication that the site nearer to the Temple is preferable since that is where G-d has chosen to rest His Name."

And so, the nearer site was decided upon. The members of the Meah Shearim Corporation bought the plot, measuring twenty-five thousand square cubits, for twenty-nine-thousand-and-sixty-eight Turkish *grush*.

Land Costs

One of the ways by which land is acquired is through money. Jerusalem real estate was no exception save that the word *"damim"* in Hebrew had to be taken by both its meanings, that is, "money" and "blood." The closer a transaction seemed to completion, the more owners cropped up with claims on it, both real and fictitious, all of whom had to be pacified and compensated, or else the Turkish authorities deleted the buyer's name from the official registry.

Suffering of this sort was painful, but the pain was eased by frequency. Jerusalem Jews were long since inured to obstructions of this type, surfacing and recurring, so that their impact was already blunted. That is, until a new trouble threatened not only to paralyze and undermine their entire project but to endanger the heads of the group.

This is how it happened:

Near the site upon which Meah Shearim was finally built, on the plot which is today occupied by the *beith knesseth* of the Bucharest *Kolel*, there lived a German missionary who conducted missionary activities in the area. This man owned a large vineyard in which he employed many Arab workers, one of whom owned a tiny plot adjacent to the lot acquired by the *shchuna* corporation. When the missionary learned of this, he began pressuring his worker not to sell his land to the Jews, for fear that this would impinge upon his territory and call a halt to his activities. He offered this worker a double salary, conditional on his refusal to sell to the Jews.

This Arab did, indeed, give his word not to sell his land and to convince his relatives to do likewise. Surreptitiously, however, he began dealing with the Jews, pressing upon his relatives to follow suit and quickly finalize the sales, knowing that such an offer would never present itself through any other source. The German was not fooled by his laborer, however, and plotted to get rid of him altogether. One time, when they were alone in the vineyard, he attacked him, stabbing him to death. He then covered the corpse over with a mound of earth to hide all traces of the vile deed.

He was not satisfied with one murder, however, and circulated the rumor that the act had been perpetrated by Jewish hands in revenge for the Arab's refusal to sell. This rumor spread as if on wings. All of the people in the missing man's village came en masse before the Turkish pasha, demanding revenge. They demanded that the murderer be apprehended immediately, otherwise, they would take the law into their own hands with a holy *jihad* war to avenge the spilled blood of their countryman. The Arab's chief suspect was none other than Rabbi Yoshe Rivlin himself, famous for his activities on the expansion front.

The pasha, who was well acquainted with Rabbi Yoshe and the Jewish community, realized immediately that their hands could not possibly have spilled this blood. This blood libel had been invented by factions wishing to sabotage the new Jewish *shchuna*. Nevertheless, he feared the Arabs, knowing that they would carry out their threats if the real murderer was not found. He therefore sent a special messenger to warn Rabbi Yoshe of what to expect, advising him to leave the city, if not the country. The English consul, responsible for Rabbi Yoshe who was an English subject, was also of the same opinion.

Rabbi Yoshe knew that their advice was sound and the threat not an empty one. He finally found himself a hideout in an abandoned Jerusalem ruin. He simultaneously hired a Jerusalem Jew famous for his astuteness, Reb Yaakov Dovid Slotkin, to serve as his liaison by informing him of the news in the city and by providing him with basic needs.

Reb Yaakov Dovid guarded his secret carefully. Aside from several noted Jerusalem figures, no one knew of Rabbi Yoshe's whereabouts or even of his existence. It was as if he had been swallowed up into the ground. Several of Rabbi Yoshe's opponents seized his disappearance as the perfect opportunity to spread the rumor that he had absconded with the corporation's funds and gone abroad. Since the secret of his whereabouts was known to very few, the natural law that slander finds a way into people's hearts was demonstrated here. The city rocked with the news. The corporation members and their families stormed the committee quarters, demanding their precious savings. They almost succeeded in doing what the Arabs threatened—quashing all plans for building the Meah Shearim complex.

From the Earth Shall Spring Forth Truth

The sound of fury in the camp of the prospective settlers reached Rabbi Yoshe's ears via his liaison man. Fearing that his entire dream would go up in smoke, he sent a beseeching letter to the Kalisher genius, Rav Meir Auerbach, who served then as the chief Rabbi of the city, pleading that he do everything in his power to publicize the truth and not let the foundations of the *shchuna* crumble altogether.

Rav Meir Auerbach secluded himself in his room and, fasting, prayed to *Hashem* that the new settlement of Meah Shearim become firmly established. On the following day, he emerged and sent word by messenger to Rabbi Yoshe and to the other members of the corporation that he was confident that by the end of the week the truth would come to light and justice would be meted out to the true murderer.

The *Gaon* of Kalish enjoyed a reputation of being a holy man and his word the word of G-d. His statement spread quickly all over the city and the public eagerly awaited further developments.

Days came and went. After five days, the pasha, accompanied by his entourage, paid a visit to the German missionary's vineyard to purchase some grapes, as he was accustomed to do each year, for the former's grapes were known for their superior quality. Whenever the ruler came, the German would take him on a grand tour of the vineyard so that he could pick out the most luscious, succulent clusters. The ruler would point out which he favored, and the Arab workers would hasten to harvest those indicated and pack them up. Meanwhile, the ruler and his host would relax in one of the thatched booths.

Upon this visit, while waiting for his grapes, the pasha suddenly jumped up from his seat and cried out, "I smell a corpse!"

He pointed to a mound of earth opposite them. "This was not here on all my past visits. That mound is the source of the disgusting smell."

The group approached the mound to inspect it more closely. The smell now struck them full force.

"Ya, Ahmad!" the pasha turned to one of the workers. "Take apart that pile of earth and let us see what is buried underneath."

To the astonishment of the group, within minutes Ahmad had uncovered the body of his lost friend and fellow laborer. As if this evidence was not enough, right nearby they found a letter addressed to the vineyard owner, proof that it had fallen out of his pocket whilst the German missionary had been preoccupied with his evil act.

In the light of such circumstantial evidence, the German could no longer stand up to the pasha's grilling interrogation. He confessed to the offensive crime and was hanged that very day.

It was now safe for Rabbi Yoshe to emerge from his hideout. The city marveled at the Kalisher *gaon*'s saintliness.

The *Gaon* of Kalish did not stand by the Meah Shearim endeavor in spirit alone. He also donated his time and money to help the project flourish, even serving as the corporation's figurehead. It was rumored that the Kalisher rabbi had brought a considerable sum along with him when he immigrated; some sources even quoted an exact figure. This did not consist of gifts, which the *rav* was known to despise. Rather, it was money he had received from his wife's dowry and which, invested with a partner, had not only grown enough to be able to support him throughout his life, but had even increased sufficiently to make him a wealthy man.

When the first stage of homes had been built in the Meah Shearim complex, the corporation trustees were forced to seek a large loan. They found a person willing to underwrite it; all he required was the guarantee of a well known person of means. Reb Shlomo Baharan turned to the Rabbi of Kalish, asking for his signature.

"In return for what?" Rav Meir asked.

Reb Shlomo Zalman and Rabbi Yoshe, who accompanied him, both opened their eyes in astonishment at this question.

"What I meant was, what price must I pay to merit such a worthy *mitzva* as the rebuilding of Jerusalem?" he explained.

"If the *rav* donates a sum equal to the numerical value of his name, Meir—that is, two-hundred-and-fifty-one lira—it will be a handsome price," replied Reb Shlomo Zalman.

"I accept!" exclaimed the Rabbi of Kalish. "And I add the identical sum to the actual construction fund."

"In that case," replied Rabbi Yoshe, "the *rav* is donating a sum equal to the numerical value of the asker, Shlomo Zalman, which equals five-hundred-and-two!"

Meah Shearim Shall Be Built with *Chessed*

The saintly Rav Nachum of Shadik was renowned not only for his greatness in Torah, but for his great holiness to the extent that people insisted that he enjoyed frequent visitations from Eliyahu Hanavi. When he left the rabbinate in Shadik, Poland, to emigrate to Eretz Yisrael, he attracted the cream of Jerusalem talent and intellect. Tens of young men in their twenties and thirties gathered around him day and night, drawing fully from his wellsprings of Torah and piety. This privilege was not available to all; one had first to sate himself upon *Shas* and *poskim*, Torah and piety before being accepted to the select circle.

Among this elite company, numbered one particular youthful student by the name of Berel, who was all of fourteen years old when he first joined Rav Nachum's circle. Although possessing a brilliant, astute mind, his fear of G-d surpassed his genius considerably. His modesty and reticence were exemplary; a mask of simplicity hid his true nature. The Jerusalem public could not fathom why this particular youngster deserved the distinction of numbering among Rav Nachum's disciples. They supposed that the reason lay in Rav Nachum's kindliness and good heart, for Berel was doubly orphaned. Rav Nachum was probably fulfilling our Sage's suggestion that the rabbi of a city take an interest in its orphans. Those close to the rabbi knew, however, that the true reason lay in Berel's intrinsic worth, in what Berel possessed and not what he lacked. Rav Nachum was wont to praise and value the boy's blessed talents and his pure piety, but most of all, he singled out the main traits that he found in Berel, the very traits which deceived and escaped the public—his modesty, humility and reticence.

After Rav Nachum's death, Berel continued studying in his *yeshiva*, led now by the great rabbi's son, who was none other than our friend Rav Zalman Baharan. Like his father, he too valued Berel's qualities.

When Berel reached marriageable age, eighteen, he became engaged to a fine, young girl. The accustomed twelve month period during which the bride makes the necessary preparations for the wedding passed, and then some weeks, but the couple still had not reached the *chuppa*. The *mechutan* threatened that if the *chathan* did not fulfill his monetary obligations of providing his own apparel for *Shabbath* and for weekday, he would call the match off.

What could Berel do? He was all alone. His modesty and meekness would not allow him to divulge his predicament to anyone.

Reb Zalman, however, realized that the preparation period had passed and his beloved *talmid* was still unmarried. Inquiring into the matter, he learned of the youth's difficult situation. And if Reb Zalman himself was unable to finance the expenses from his own pocket, he was, after all, a veteran *askan*. Was not the one who solicited charity greater than one who actually gave it? Especially so in the case of *hachnassath kalla*!

When Reb Zalman Baharan decided to undertake any great *mitzva*, it was guaranteed to be performed completely, in a superlative fashion. At this point, he approached his cousin who bore the same name, Rabbi Zalman Baharil ben HaRav Yaakov Leib Levi and together they formulated a plan to secure the necessary missing funds.

"Actually, I had been wondering for some time now why

Berel was not getting married," said his cousin. "I meant to ask you about it."

"Very well," Reb Zalman said. "Listen to my idea, and if it pleases you and finds favor in *Hashem's* eyes, we may have the solution for raising the money without applying to the depleted *tzedaka* coffers of the city, and without causing Berel embarrassment."

"How is that?" asked Rabbi Zalman Baharil.

"We have just purchased land for the Meah Shearim *shchuna*, enough to build one-hundred-and-ten units. This year we will surely not build more than twenty. If so, let us plant wheat on the remaining land to be specially preserved under our supervision from the harvest on and used for *shmura matza*. The profits of this venture will be set aside for *hachnassath kalla*. Thus Berel will not be dipping into any funds set aside for other charities."

How marvelous is the conversation of wise men of action who fulfill the verse, "Then did the pious consult together." Not only is their conversation brief and their deeds numerous, but their agreement is speedily converted into action. Thus it was with the two Zalmans. Finding no objections or flaws in their idea, they did not delay lest the *mitzva* sour on them. Within the hour they were already walking towards the site of their conversation, to Meah Shearim. Shortly later, their hems tucked into their belts, their hands were busy clearing away the many stones scattered throughout the area.

Passersby seeing them thus, nodded knowingly at them, assuming that the plans for the Meah Shearim housing complex had been tabled, that it was still a mere dream. Apparently, even the funds to clear the ground and dig foundations were lacking, and the rabbis had to resort to digging with their own bare hands.

46

The Zalmans paid no attention to the whisperings and winkings directed at them and behind their backs. They labored diligently, clearing away, smoothing, plowing and planting the area with wheat. Within days, G-d sent His blessing in the form of plentiful rain, and the do-gooders saw that He had approved of their labor.

That very week, the two Zalmans visited the *mechutan* to prod him to begin the wedding preparations, guaranteeing to pay Berel's share of the expenses, as promised at the *tenaim* ceremony. They also borrowed enough to clothe Berel handsomely, secure in their conviction that they would be able to repay their debts in time.

Not long after, the wedding was celebrated in full splendor. The joy was complete. The two Zalmans actively participated in gladdening the *chathan* and *kalla*, dancing before them for hours on end. They also managed to repay their debts before Pesach, for the land produced golden sheaves laden with heavy kernels, which were the source of that year's *matzoth* for the Jerusalem population.

And so, the land upon which Meah Shearim was to stand produced its first crop, a crop of charity and kindness to gladden the hearts of an orphan and lead him to the *chuppa*.

Hashem, the Builder of Jerusalem

Jerusalem Jewry saw the founding fathers of Meah Shearim as three: Reb Zalman Baharan, Rabbi Yoshe Rivlin and Rabbi Ben Zion Leon. From the beginning steps until the end, these three spared none of their time, money or energies to assure the success of the project. They were to be found on the building site at all hours of the day, Reb Zalman in particular, who shouldered responsibility for everything, from the foundation to the roof.

During the period of excavation, the English consul accompanied by his aide, appeared one day, when the three *askanim* were present. The consul, who was acquainted with them all from previous dealings, informed the *askanim* that he had been asked by Sir Montefiore to visit the site of the Meah Shearim project and give him a detailed report of developments there—who headed the corporation, where the exact location was and mainly, what were the group's financial resources.

"The primary source," the three answered in unison, "is faith, as it is written, 'The builder of Jerusalem is G-d.' We are only fulfilling His will. All we are required to do is to commence; the rest will surely be completed through heavenly Providence."

"With what resources have you begun the work?" asked the gentile consul.

"With pennies," was the reply.

"From where did you get these pennies?"

"Every member of the corporation has invested from his own pocket," the three men answered.

"Despite the fact that most of you are paupers?" the consul pressed. "If you are really doing what is right, if this is truly the will of G-d, why does G-d not open His treasury and shower you with wealth?"

"He is testing us. We are certain that if we withstand the trial and faithfully carry out His design, we will lack nothing."

"And what will you do if one of the members regrets his

involvement? This is, after all, much like a wild dream!" the consul pressed on.

"Whoever wishes to withdraw his membership may do so and will receive his investment back. But we have already seen that when one person backs out, two others appear to take his place."

The answers of the three pleased the consul, who promised to support them to the best of his ability. And, indeed, this gentile stood by them whenever the need arose and whenever he was approached by the three for assistance.

One Who Seeks—Finds

Our Sages say that the original *chassidim*, men of piety and holiness, were blessed in that their *chassidic* practices caused their Torah knowledge to be preserved. When was this true? When all their leisure time was utilized for Torah, for then heaven assisted them by combining their labor in *Chassiduth* with their labor in Torah, augmenting it and making a non-interrupted unity of the whole. For if one seeks, one shall find.

Reb Zalman, whom we have seen continually absorbed with the needs of others, helping arrange support for a widow, encouraging a lonely person and the like, could have had all of his time consumed. In addition, he bore the public responsibility upon his shoulders, being a central figure in the Jerusalem community, to say nothing of the Meah Shearim settlement project of which he was the vibrant spirit. Yet, despite all, he was never too preoccupied to take advantage of every single spare minute for intensive Torah study.

One never saw Reb Zalman emerge from his house without a *seifer* under his arm, be it a *Gemara, Mishnayoth*, Rambam, work of the *rishonim*, commentary of the *acharonim* or the notebook in which he would jot down some Torah innovation which occurred to him on the spur of the moment. At all odd moments in the midst of his work, he would burrow deeply into a *seifer*, writing his comments into the notebook.

Indeed, in his folio of innovations, we often find him commenting that some idea or another had struck him at the building site or in the pasha's waiting room.

Reb Zalman might be in the middle of giving a lecture to his *talmidim* involved in some intricate matter, when he would be called to come to the aid of some solitary widow who had taken ill. Upon the doctor's recommendation, she had been removed to the Bikur Cholim hospital. However, she had not had any funds to cover the admittance fee. What was to be done? Someone would suddenly recall that Reb Zalman was the *gabbai* of Bikur Cholim; he would surely be able to help out. Reb Zalman would not hesitate. Neither would he trust messenger or letter. He himself would go down to the hospital administrator to arrange the widow's admission, after which he would continue to keep a protective eye on her until she recuperated.

From the hospital, he would return to his lecture and, wonder of wonders, the difficult *sugya* would suddenly become so crystal clear that his *talmidim* would be at a loss to explain why they had not understood the matter beforehand. They would be convinced that their *rebbe* had been enlightened with the true explanation in the merit of the *mitzva* he had just performed.

Sensing their thoughts intuitively, Reb Zalman would demur,

"No, my *talmidim*. Our Sages taught that there is no reward for *mitzva* performance in this world. The reward of understanding a *sugya* comes only with effort. For all the time that I spent in the hospital, I did not let my mind wander for a moment from our topic, until I found the right explanation. That is the meaning of the adage, 'If one has labored and found—believe him!'"

People used to tell another story about Reb Zalman. He was once discussing a topic in *Gemara* when one of his *talmidim* posed a difficult question. Before Reb Zalman had time to think about it, the door opened and a Turkish officer entered with a summons for him to appear immediately before the ruler.

Reb Zalman quickly donned his outer coat and, as usual, stuffed a small *Gemara* under his arm. After staying in the ruler's house for several hours, he returned to his *shi'ur*, answer in hand. His *talmidim* were astounded. How could their *rebbe* have hit upon such a clever solution? Surely in the ruler's house he had not had any opportunity to even open the *Gemara*!

"Do not be surprised, my dear *talmidim*," he explained. "Don't you know that I do not speak Turkish? My exchange with the pasha is always held in Arabic, which the ruler does not understand. In the intervals of translation by the interpreter, I found precious moments to ponder the question until I finally came up with the correct solution."

The Miracle of the First Night

From the first steps of the Meah Shearim corporation until the project was completed, it was clear that a Heavenly Hand was guiding the construction. Indeed, the founders suffered their measure of trials, pains and setbacks, but with the mercy of Heaven they overcame them all, emerging steeled from the forge to seize a firm hold which no wind could shake.

As already mentioned, Meah Shearim had three founding fathers: Rabbi Yoshe Rivlin and Reb Zalman Baharan, the initiators and originators, of whom much has already been told, and a third one, Rabbi Ben Zion Leon, whose money and efforts were instrumental in seeing the project through. At the first general assembly of the corporation, every member laid out one small Turkish coin as a nominal deposit. Rabbi Ben Zion, present at the initial meeting, also gave his coin. When the assembly dispersed, however, he approached Reb Zalman.

"Do not worry, Reb Zalman," he said. "I will go with you to every negotiation for land purchase, and whatever sum you lack I will meet from my own pocket."

Rabbi Ben Zion was a man of his word. After the deal was completed, and every member was required to produce an additional two Turkish lira, the treasury contained twenty-three thousand five-hundred-and-seventeen *grush*. The missing seven thousand *grush* was donated by Rabbi Ben Zion from his own pocket.

The original plan for Meah Shearim called for erecting one hundred units within ten years, or ten units per year. But with the help of *Hashem*, all one hundred apartments were completed within six years, from 5634-41 (1874-81).

The architect, secretary, treasurer and engineer of the complex, the person who collected the funds and hired labor, was none other than Reb Zalman Baharan, who was the sole authority and executive, the first and last word. And G-d was with him.

On Chanuka of 5635 (1875), the first ten apartments were assigned by drawing lots. Numbering among the first winners, who immediately transferred to the new quarters, was Rabbi Asher Anshel Neiman, Rabbi of Vitsein and author of *Keren Ben Shamen*, who left his rabbinical position in Hungary in the year 5621 (1861), and emigrated with his wife and small children to Jerusalem.

Rabbi Asher Anshel was well known in Hungary for his righteousness and brilliance and was particularly beloved by the leaders of his generation, the saintly Chatham Sofer and the Gri Assad. Upon his immigration to the Holy City, he numbered among the elite of the city and the guardians of its fortress. He was among the founders of Kolel Ungarin and Shomrei Hachomoth, and among the foremost opponents of the *maskilim* who were then attempting to infiltrate into the Holy Land with the intent to establish secular schools.

His settling in the new *shchuna* added much stature to the project outside the walls and increased the flow of Jews from Jerusalem to its outer suburbs. (Rabbi Asher Anshel died in 5642 and was buried in the section of the great men of Jerusalem, between the graves of Rav Avraham Shag and Rav Meir Auerbach, author of *Imrei Bina*.)

Reb Zalman was not among the first winners of the lottery. Nevertheless, he joined the settlers upon their first night in the new compound, understanding that his presence would help dispel the fear that gripped the settlers at the prospect of sleeping outside of the protective city wall.

Who knows what would have happened had Reb Zalman not made this decision? Who knows how things would have turned out if not for his presence? Towards evening, one of Reb Yitzchak Nachum Levi's children stepped out of his house, slipped and was bitten on the finger by a scorpion. The child screamed in pain, drawing all the settlers to Reb Yitzchak Nachum's house. There they all stood, helpless. There was no doctor in the compound. To rush the child back to the city was not feasible, both because of the dangerous transit and because the city gates were locked at night. Meanwhile, the child was writhing in pain, perhaps dying. Everyone stood around, wringing hands in desperation and sighing hopelessly.

The only one who did not lose his wits was Reb Zalman. He put the child's finger into his own mouth and began sucking vigorously until his entire mouth was filled with blood. The venom, however, was ejected together with the blood. The poison must have been extremely potent, for as soon as it entered Reb Zalman's mouth, he became suffused with a cold sweat. But even though he had endangered himself, Reb Zalman was certain that no harm would befall him, for he had saved the life of a Jewish child and, together with it, the future of the settlement.

Once the poison was out, the child quieted down. Reb Zalman then asked each person to return home while he remained to watch over the child, in case he should require further attention. Throughout that entire night, Reb Zalman did not cease reciting *Tehillim* and praying that no further mishap occur, G-d forbid.

By dawn, the child was completely healed. His pain was

gone and he felt fine. Reb Zalman made the rounds to all the settlers to tell them the good news.

A Diminutive Sanctuary in the New City

The Meah Shearim settlement project was only a step in the expansion of the *yishuv* in Eretz Yisrael and the rebuilding of Jerusalem. When ten Jews arrive in a new city, their first concern is that G-d rest His Presence in their midst. It was, therefore, necessary to provide a house for Torah study and worship which would radiate light upon its entire establishment.

"Have you ever seen ten Jews without their synagogue?" Reb Zalman asked the members at the general gathering that took place before they took possession of their homes. To be sure, there were many other things the pioneer settlers lacked, ranging from shoelaces to fruit and vegetables. All such things had to be brought from the city within the walls. Even the improved living conditions, within the relatively spacious houses, did not dispel the feeling of wilderness. Foxes still roamed freely about the *shchuna*. The sounds of wailing coyotes could be heard at night, and snakes and scorpions abounded. It was dangerous to leave a door or window open even by day, lest uninvited guests find their way into the house.

This did not deter the pioneer "Nachshons." What disturbed them primarily was the lack of place for Torah study and prayer.

On the ninth of Kislev, 5635 (1875), some three weeks before the lottery was cast to determine the first ten settlers, the Jews of Jerusalem gathered to lay the cornerstone for the first *beith knesseth* in Meah Shearim. To this very day it remains the sections's largest, the Yeshuoth Yaakov synagogue.

The name was given by Reb Zalman Baharan who saw in this building as well, the salvation of *Hashem*. A wealthy, G-d-fearing Jew, Reb Yosef Yehoshua ben Rabbi Yaakov of Tranow and his wife Yente, happened to be visiting Jerusalem just at this time. They were a childless couple. A brief talk with Reb Zalman was sufficient to convince Reb Yosef to establish the Meah Shearim *beith knesseth* on his father's name.

All of the Jerusalem population—men, women and children—attended the cornerstone laying foundation. It was an impressive show of force, expressing the feelings of the entire public at the historic breaking-through-the-walls and the expansion of the *yishuv*.

Even the noted personalities of the city attended, led by Rav Meir Auerbach of Kalish. This elderly scholar was very moved by the occasion and instructed that the list of the ten original settlers be transcribed on parchment and placed in a glass container for safekeeping as a record for posterity. This receptacle was to be preserved by embedding it into the very foundation of the building.

He also announced, upon this occasion, his donation towards the women's section of the synagogue, besides a considerable sum for the construction of a magnificent *bima* platform The joy and enthusiasm so prevalent and evident in the atmosphere were like a stamp of approval for the participants, like a seal of certification that here indeed would be erected a lighthouse beacon whose light would guide the coming generations.

The founder of the synagogue, Reb Yosef Yehoshua, was himself so moved by the general jubilation and the realization that this edifice would serve as a center of Torah study and worship for generations, that he stood up, announcing the doubling of his original grant. This money was later used to build an additional hall and six rooms for prayer, west of the main synagogue, to serve as classrooms for a *cheider*.

These prayer rooms are still being used today as the *shtiblach* of Meah Shearim. The number of *mithpallilim* which they daily attract, morning and evening, is perhaps unequalled anywhere in the world!

Those Who Do Not Return Insults

Parnassim of our people, who have throughout the ages dedicated their lives to the public welfare, know by experience that among those benefiting from their efforts and reaping from their labors, they will always find individuals ready to bury them under an avalanche of complaints and eager to sharpen their tongues against them. This is all the more true in Jerusalem, except that not every *askan* is equipped with a reservoir of humility and self-effacement as Reb Zalman Baharan was. Here is a case in point.

When the Meah Shearim settlement began stirring with its first signs of life, it already numbered over one hundred sponsors or family heads. The sewage system had by then outgrown its original design and required a thorough overhaul. This entailed considerable outlay of funds, half of which the "city council" or the "*shchuna* corporation" provided and the other half of which was to be divided among the dwellers, since each home would be connected to the new network. All logical and simple, on the surface. But this appeared so only to one not directly involved in the matter. One of the homeowners, a man of considerable means and considerable miserliness, owned three homes in the complex. According to his warped logic the cost should have been divided according to the total number of homeowners rather than per unit.

This man ran into Reb Zalman in the marketplace one day and let loose a string of oaths and denunciations for having been triply charged.

Reb Zalman shrugged his shoulders, stepped aside and continued on his way. "Far better people than he lost their sense over money matters," he said to himself. "Why should I take offense? Our Sages said that a person's true nature can be determined by his attitude to his pocket. Sometimes, the purse can make a person lose his very humanity. A person should not be judged in his time of trouble, all the more so if his trouble is financial." And so, Reb Zalman pitied the man and overlooked the slight.

If this man had cursed Reb Zalman in private, no one would have learned of it, certainly not from Reb Zalman himself who had not even felt the sting. Since it happened in public, in the middle of the marketplace, before countless witnesses, the matter reached the ears of the *shchuna* rabbis, among them Rabbi Shaul Chaim Horowitz, former Rabbi of Dobrovna, who indignantly championed the honor of so great a *talmid chacham* and *tzaddik* as Reb Zalman.

He formally ostracized the *shchuna* resident for having shamed a *talmid chacham*. The decree would be in effect until he accepted his rebuke in public and sought forgiveness for his sin.

All of the residents of Meah Shearim were summoned that very day to the Yeshuoth Yaakov synagogue, the ostracized man amongst them. The latter came unshod. As he passed through the crowd, it receded a full four cubits, as the *halacha* requires. The man walked up to the central platform and in sobbing voice, confessed his shameful act of abusing a *talmid chacham*. Then he begged forgiveness for his sin.

To the sinner's dismay, Reb Zalman was not amongst the crowd, not knowing anything of the matter, just as he had not been aware that he had been insulted.

When Reb Zalman learned of the event, after the crowd had already dispersed, he was deeply disturbed by the anguish that had been caused to a fellow Jew through him. His *talmidim* found him upset and overwrought. Reb Zalman begged them to accompany him, and before long, others had joined the procession as well. The swelling group followed Reb Zalman towards that man's house.

When the ostracized man looked out his window and saw Reb Zalman approaching, tailed by a huge crowd, he did not know what to make of it. Had he not accepted his rebuke publicly, as had been required to do? What did Reb Zalman want of him now? Why was he descending so solemnly upon the house, leading such a procession?

Before long, there came a polite knock on the door. Reb Zalman entered, followed by his entourage, weeping loudly and wringing his hands in grief.

"It was all my fault, dear brother. I am to blame for your having insulted me today. I surely bear you no grudge, for you did nothing. I am begging you to forgive me!"

Reb Zalman left with two accomplishments. That Jew

kissed his hand and donated the full sum necessary for the entire community's new sewage system. And, from then on, he became one of the settlement's chief supporters.

The *Beith Din* Sits on *Motza'ey Shabbath*

It was *Motza'ey Shabbath*, the twenty-fifth of Adar, 5660. Jerusalem Jewry noticed the *beith din shamash* hastening in his horse-drawn wagon to round up the city *dayanim* for the meeting which was to take place in the Churva *shul* courtyard.

It was rare for the *beith din* to convene at night, all the more, for a special session to which Rav Yosef Chayim Sonnenfeld had also been summoned even though he did not as yet number among the regular *dayanim*. It was stranger still that the meeting had been called for *Motza'ey Shabbath*. No one could recall a precedent for it.

What had happened?

The founder and builder of Meah Shearim, the great, righteous Reb Zalman Baharan had just died in the Bikur Cholim Hospital. According to ancient tradition, based upon an amendment of *Chazal*, it was forbidden to let a body remain unburied overnight within the Holy City. Knowing how beloved Reb Zalman had been to the entire Jerusalem population—men, women, and children alike—the city leaders feared that the congestion and crush guaranteed for a funeral that size would be especially dangerous at night. They were therefore gathering to discuss the matter and to perhaps allow for a postponement of the *tzaddik's* funeral until morning. It was, they felt, truly a matter of *pikuach nefesh*, the preservation of life.

Reb Zalman had never asked anything of anyone during his lifetime; so too in his death he had no demands to make of his offspring in his will. The only request he had before his soul departed, and even this was suggested after much apology, was that if he died in the hospital, he wished his family to observe the seven days of mourning in the hospital rather than at home.

This was also a topic under consideration by the *beith din*— should the time-worn Jerusalem custom of observing the *shiv'a* in the deceased's home be suspended? The *beith din* gave in to this, too.

Reb Zalman's outstanding, typifying trait throughout his life was that of *chessed*. His entire being was enveloped, enmeshed in *chessed*, even in his last days. Throughout his illness, he lay in the corridor. Why? Reb Zalman had always reviewed his study aloud. This habit was all the more important to him during his illness for, as our Sages taught, "Torah studied aloud is not easily forgotten" (*Eruvin* 54), and as King Solomon taught, "Torah is life-sustaining to all who seek it and a cure for their flesh." Fearing that his voice would disturb the other patients, Reb Zalman decided to remain in the corridor.

There was another reason as well. As soon as he felt the slightest relief from his tremendous suffering, Reb Zalman would get out of bed and visit the other patients and the staff and perform small services for them. "The patients certainly need attention," Reb Zalman would say. "As for the workers, they are exhausted from their taxing work."

This was Reb Zalman, to his dying day when he was summoned to the *yeshiva shel ma'ala*. This was how he had lived his life within his *shchuna*, the Meah Shearim city.

His outer aspect and his inner being demonstrated truth. He

was one flaming torch of truth. And like a precious stone completing a royal crown, with the last breath he exhaled while alive, he uttered the word "*emes.*"

Throughout that last *Shabbath*, Reb Zalman's soul was split, half here and half in the world beyond. He tried, with superhuman strength, to hold on to his soul throughout that *Shabbath* so as not to mar the holy day for his descendants and friends, praying that his soul cleave to his body until after *havdala*.

After *havdala* had been recited in his presence, that *Motza'ey Shabbath*, Reb Zalman asked for a *kezayith* of *challa* to fulfill his *melave malke* obligation. After he had recited *Birchath Hamazon*, he called his offspring and friends to him, saying the *Shema*, word for word, together with the gathering. Then, even though it was nighttime, he gathered his *tzitzith* in his hand and kissed them. When he reached the phrase, "*Hashem Elokeichem emes*," his soul expired with the last word.

The flame of truth ascended to heaven. The great *tzaddik*, Reb Zalman Baharan, builder of Jerusalem, had been summoned to the heavenly city of Jerusalem and was mourned by the Jerusalem populace for many, many days.

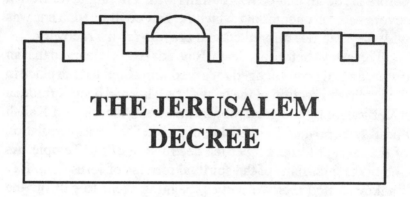

THE JERUSALEM DECREE

The Jerusalem Genius Dances at a Wedding

It was the twenty-second of Sivan, 5668 (1908). Throngs of Jerusalem Jews marched, mourning and broken-hearted, after the bier of the Jerusalem *tzaddik* Rav Yaakov Orenstein who had passed away suddenly at the prime age of forty-nine.

All store shutters were down, for the *beith din* had announced a general cessation of work. *Talmud Torah* children, let out of school, swarmed en masse in the procession. Jerusalem giants ascended one after another to the rostrum to eulogize the deceased and depict the community's great loss. Among them was the deceased's father, the great Rav Yeshaya, who at the conclusion of his dirge gave a bitter shout: "He was my only son; he was an only one in his generation."

The death of Rav Yaakov Orenstein came as a sudden blow to the Jews of Jerusalem. They had not known the three days before his death that he was burning with a raging fever from a severe case of pneumonia which he had contracted. That was why they had not offered special prayers for his recovery.

Three days before his death, Rav Yaakov had learned that an orchestra had been engaged for a wedding about to take place in the Bucharim section of the New City. This had been forbidden in Jerusalem by the great rabbis Rav Meir Auerbach of Kalish and Rav Yehoshua Leib Diskin of Brisk, for it was a violation of the precept to remember the destruction of the Temple. As one of the guardians of the spiritual fortress of Jerusalem, Rav Yaakov visited the two parties, begging them to call off the orchestra, which they did.

Fearing however, that by his act he had diminished the joy of the bride and groom on which our Sages had placed such emphasis, he came to the wedding where he danced unceasingly for two hours to gladden the hearts of all present. He left the hall dripping perspiration and arrived home with a severe case of pneumonia. Three days later his precious soul ascended to heaven.

The Sons of Jerusalem

Rav Yaakov Orenstein was the pride of Jerusalem. Born in the Old City to his renowned father Rav Yeshaya in 5619 (1859), he exhibited extraordinary talents while still a child. He received his early education from his father and from his grandfather, Rav Uri Orenstein, son-in-law of the author of *Keren Orah* and one of the prime disciples of the Lubavitcher Rebbe, the Tzemach Tzeddek.

When the child grew up, he became a member of Rav Meir

64

Auerbach's household, and it was from him that he learned the basic precepts of Torah. At the age of sixteen he married Tzipora, the stepdaughter of the Rabbi of Jerusalem, Rav Shmuel Salant. He thus formed an attachment to Rav Shmuel, who taught him *Halachic* procedure.

The appearance of Rav Yehoshua Leib Diskin of Brisk at Jerusalem's gates was the signal for all the sharp minds in the holy city to converge and form a solid group around that *tzaddik*. Rav Yaakov, who was then only eighteen years old, became one of the outstanding scholars of this elite and sanctified group, eventually becoming the acknowledged star disciple.

In his writings, Rav Yaakov describes this period of study under the *Gaon* of Brisk:

"From the time I viewed the rays of light emanating from his sanctified face, I did not leave his tent; I did not move from his pure home until the very last moment. I will not lie to my own soul by referring to myself as a *talmid*, knowing full well that greater and better men than I did not achieve such stature. He had the power to bring to light sixty-three marvelous insights upon one page of *Gemara* and *Tosfoth*, all radically different one from the other, yet without exhibiting any encyclopedic feats, everything quite simple and logical and in one place. There has been no one to compare with him from the times of the authors of the *Urim Vetumim*, the *Sh'agath Arye* and Rabbi Akiba Eger. During his first six months in Eretz Yisrael he delivered a lecture to the incisive minds of the Holy City for four consecutive hours daily, nonstop, even on Fridays and *motza'ey Shabbatot*, only omitting *Erev Yom Kippur*. This missing lesson he completed on the evening of *Yom Kippur* after the *Maariv* service. We used to look at one another, marveling at the vast wisdom with which G-d had blessed His devout follower."

Rav Yaakov was a most talented person. Many stories were told of his prowess in mathematics and other sciences, but all this was wholly insignificant compared with his accomplishments in Torah. All worldly matters were of no import to him whatsoever.

His wife once saw him get up during the night, wash his hands briskly and eagerly and break out into a rousing dance. The woman grew frightened, but Rav Yaakov hurried to explain that he had been pondering over a difficult matter for several days. That night, however, he had been visited by Rabbi Akiba Eger who explained the difficulty to him. He had not been able to contain his excitement and had broken out into a dance. Rav Yaakov then vowed that if Hashem blessed him with a son within that year he would name the child Akiba. A son was indeed born within the year, and Rav Yaakov fulfilled his vow, but the child subsequently died before his thirteenth year.

Another time, on his way to the *yeshiva*, one of his shoes fell off, but in his extreme absorption in his study, even along the way, he did not perceive the loss. He arrived at the *yeshiva* with one unshod foot.

One night he returned from the *yeshiva* and sat down to supper. Intending to pour a little oil on his plate into which to dip his meager portion of bread, Rav Yaakov took the kerosene can instead and ate his bread dipped in that liquid without remarking the difference. He then returned to his studies in the *beith midrash* until midnight.

What prompted a personality so sublime that his every thought was intertwined in Torah study to close his *Gemara* and go to dance at a wedding of people whom he did not even know, to the extent of risking his own health and life?

RETURN TO THE HEAVENLY CITY

A Plague in the Holy City

The years of 5625-6 (1865-6) were difficult for the Jerusalem settlement which had been newly re-established after the long, desolate gap caused by the exile of the Jewish people. Cholera ran rampant, strewing corpses in the dozens. The settlement dwindled. This period was a critical one for many Jews who had emigrated from the Diaspora at tremendous self-sacrifice, having endured weeks-long journeys by sea in sailing vessels. This critical period broke their strong will to relocate themselves on the land. They returned to their homes in the exile, broken, crushed and in dire poverty.

The families remaining inside the city walls desperately fanned the flickers of hope and encouragement sparked by the Jerusalem leaders who would not allow the settlers to fall into the arms of despair. Then came the bitter day, the third of Shevat, 5625 (1865), upon which one of the fathers of the settlement, the beloved Rav Moshe Yehuda Leib of Kutna, author of *Zayith Ra'anan* and *Tifereth Yerushalayim*, died. The frightful disease had visited his home just two days before. During these two days the Jews of Jerusalem had kept shifts of worshippers by the *Kothel* to pray for his recovery, but the gates of heaven had been sealed.

Jerusalem leaders informed the communities in the Diaspora of their dire situation. "The danger of extinction hovers over the new settlement in the Holy Land," they wrote. "Increase your prayers and please—ask *Hashem* why we were visited with this tragedy." They also aroused the Jews of Jerusalem to repentance.

Jerusalem Jews—whose very lives were sanctified and pure, whose whole world was Torah and prayer—for what did they have to repent? Rav Meir Auerbach of Kalish and Rav Shmuel Salant, the rabbi of the city, perceived this very fact as a flaw. Every single Jew in Jerusalem was a living Torah scroll. Perhaps it was this familiarity with sanctity—the very stones of the city spewed purity—that caused the inhabitants to perhaps slight one another by not exhibiting the proper awe and respect for each other. Perhaps this was the cause of the plague. The *Maggidim* increasingly mentioned the disciples of Rabbi Akiba who had been decimated by plague for not having shown the proper respect for one another.

Jerusalemites added another hour to their already exhausting schedule of study; another page of *Gemara* beyond the hundreds they were accustomed to learn. The non-Jewish physicians warned about isolating the sick for fear of contamination, but the Jews of Jerusalem did not spare themselves. They preformed merciful acts for the sick by day and by night, always looking for some way to lighten their suffering.

And indeed, by the summer of 5625 (1865), the situation improved somewhat. Many began to believe that the epidemic was tapering off, but their hopes were short lived. In the beginning of the winter of 5626 (1866) it broke out anew in full fury. The fresh graves of young Jewish victims who had lived brief but pure lives were added daily to those already standing on the Mount of Olives. The members of the *Chevra Kadisha* used to descend from the Dung Gate to the cemetery several times daily. Reports reaching the Diaspora about the dreadful state of events caused deep sorrow and distress to whomever heard the news. But there was no one who could offer a clue as to why the House of Israel should be so punished, as to the reason for this great wrath.

The sun set in midday on the third of Marcheshvan that year

when the saintly Rav Yosef Zundel of Salant was summoned to the heavenly academy. Ten days later he was followed by the great Rav Nachum of Shadik.

Rav Meir Auerbach's Dream

Rav Meir Auerbach had been visiting the house of his master, Rav Rafael Yedidya Abulafya, head of the sages of the *kabbalistic* Beith El *yeshiva*, to try to divine from him the cause behind this evil decree, but he had not succeeded. The great Rav Nachum of Shadik had himself been one of the scholars of the Beith El *yeshiva* while his brother, Rav Yaakov Leib, head of the city's *beith din*, had been a disciple of Rav Rafael Yedidya. Therefore, the tragedy of Rav Nachum's death struck the great *kabbalist* a personal blow.

In the midst of the *shiv'a*, the Rabbi of Kalish renewed his pressure on Rav Rafael Yedidya to discover by mystic methods why the Jewish settlement was being systematically wiped out.

In the time of Rav Rafael Yedidya's teacher, Rav Rafael Avraham Shalom (head of Beith El and grandson of the famed Rav Shalom Sharabi), Jerusalem had been terrorized by many bandits. For a long period people were unable to enter or leave the city. The rabbi had then told his disciple Rav Rafael Yedidya, that the troubles being visited upon Jerusalem were due to the lack of reverence shown by the settlers to the *Kothel HaMa'aravi*, the remaining segment of the Western Wall dating back to the Holy Temple. He had, however, warned his *talmid* not to reveal this secret until he received a sign from heaven to do so. He explained to his great *talmid* that if he revealed to the world the great sanctity of the *Kothel* and the

69

terrible punishment deserving of those who were not cautious enough of its holiness, all the Jews of the Diaspora would fear to come to Jerusalem.

And now Rav Rafael Yedidya could not face the pressing pleas of his own *talmid*, the Rabbi of Kalish. His heart burst at the sight of the Cedars of Lebanon being hacked down; it agonized over the knights of the Torah who had died. He delayed a positive answer until evening. The Rabbi of Kalish returned to his home, with a faint glimmer of hope in his heart.

Three hours after the *ma'ariv* prayers, Rav Meir made his way to the Beith El *yeshiva* to his regular *shi'ur* with his teacher.

"What are we to study this evening?" he asked.

"Tonight we will deal with the question of a dream query and the special thoughts one must concentrate upon when making such a query," the *rosh yeshiva* replied.

The Rabbi of Kalish understood the hint.

They finished their lesson by daybreak. The Rabbi of Kalish returned home. Between daybreak and sunup he managed to write out a reply to a complicated *halachic* question he had received, joining a copy of it to the work he was about to publish, *Imrei Bina*. He then went to the ancient *beith midrash*, Menachem Tzion, which was part of the Churva synagogue complex, to pray with the *vathikin minyan*.

After his prayers he veered from his normal practice. Instead of going home to eat a light breakfast, after which he would go on to the offices of the *beith din*, today he descended to the Shiloach spring, to the place traditionally known as the *mikveh* of Rabbi Yishmael the High Priest. There he immersed himself three hundred and ten times in purity, returning home to envelop himself again in his *tallith* and *tefillin*. One of his disciples had in the meantime left a note on the door to prevent disturbances:

"The rabbi will not receive the public today."

The Rabbi of Kalish fasted that entire day, not ceasing to study all the while. Towards evening he went again to the *mikveh, davened ma'ariv* early and recited the *Shema* before retiring, extending each word and accompanying it with much crying. All the while he kept in his mind the holy concentrations of the Arizal which his teacher had submitted to him. He prepared the dream query according to his teacher's instructions, writing it in sanctity upon a piece of parchment. Then, still fasting, he lay himself down upon his bed, the parchment under his head. Just about midnight he awoke but fainted immediately. He had just seen, most vividly, in letters of black fire written upon white fire, the verse in *Shir Hashirim*, "My beloved resembles a gazelle or a fawn, behold he stands behind our wall." The members of his household who became aware of his condition rushed excitedly to arouse him. The Rabbi of Kalish washed his hands quickly, sat down and began to ponder over the vision his eyes had seen. Imagine! He had already received an answer to his question, but he could not yet decipher it. He recalled what the Sages had commented on the opening words, "Like the gazelles and the deer of the field." The Sages had read this as meaning, "Behold I will abandon your flesh like the gazelles and deer." Apparently, the rabbi thought, this is the allusion to the rampant plague. He again reviewed before his mind's eye the succeeding words engraved upon his memory, "Behold our wall." The Sages had explained this to refer to the Western Wall. Surely this was a hint that they should offer plentiful prayers at the *Kothel*.

"But how many rivers of tears have we already poured out there?" he asked himself.

Without saying a word, he wrapped himself up in his

71

overcoat and went to his teacher, Rav Rafael Yedidya. To his surprise, the *rebbe* was already awaiting him outside with a joyful smile on his face. He now told his disciple what he had heard that very midnight. A sudden commotion, afterwards a voice exclaiming, "Who divulged this secret to My sons?"

"You now surely know the reason behind the plague, Rav Meir," he said, "and I am certain that you will soon understand how to remedy the situation. May *Hashem* grant you success."

"Yes, *rebbe*," the Rabbi of Kalish replied. "I have received the answer, but I cannot translate it into action." He reviewed the verse he had seen written in fire.

Rav Rafael Yedidya informed him that he had correctly interpreted the first half of the verse, that it was indeed an allusion to the decree. Now he told him at length what he had learned from his own teacher, that the Western Wall, from which the Divine Presence had never departed, was demanding its just reverence. Our Sages had not accepted the view of the *Perushim* that one should abstain entirely from expressions of joy from the day of the destruction onward, he explained, but still one must bear in mind the warning to "Call the destruction of the Temple to mind at the height of one's rejoicing." Jerusalem Jews should be as mourners whose departed one is stretched out before them. Yet, instead, people celebrating weddings in the Holy City sing to the accompaniment of musical instruments, forgetting completely the tragedy of the destruction. The Western Wall demands its due measure of mourning; less than that is a slight to its honor.

The Rabbi of Kalish did not waste one precious moment. With a bow, he kissed his *rebbe's* hand and hurried to summon his *beith din*. Special messengers left for Rav Shmuel Salant's house and for the homes of the other Jerusalem wise men.

Within a short interval they had all converged upon the chambers of the *beith din*.

The Ban on Musical Instruments

No one knew why the Rabbi of Kalish had summoned a gathering of rabbis in these hectic days in the suffering city, at a time when no house was spared from its sick and dead. But the righteous men of Jerusalem were heedful of the command of the Kalisher Rabbi and came.

The Rabbi of Kalish left his house, his face seemingly like that of a fallen angel. Thoroughly shaken, ashenly pale, he took his place at the head of the room and between sobs told the gathering what he had seen in the previous night's dream, adding what his teacher, the great *rosh yeshiva* of Beith El, had said.

The room was absolutely still. No one had any word of encouragement or suggestion to offer to assuage the slighted pride of the Western Wall and to still the voice which rang out daily from Mount Sinai bemoaning, "Woe to Me for having destroyed My own house." Slowly the room filled with both short and drawn out sighs of Jerusalem Jews commiserating along with the Wall.

After a wordless pause, the rabbi again stood at the fore. This time he had a suggestion to offer, one at which his teacher had actually hinted. "The greatest *simcha* a Jew experiences is when he marries off one of his children," the rabbi said, "yet at the peak of his joy he must remind himself to curb it. Our Sages decreed various practices to limit this *simcha*, for example that the bridegrooms' crowns be replaced by ashes on his head, all in order to fulfill the verse, 'I shall call Jerusalem to mind at the height of my rejoicing.' Our Sages themselves did not accept all these bans which they had suggested, but that was only because no real settlement existed then in Jerusalem. But now, my friends, that Jews from the exile are gathering to Jerusalem's walls, now, in face of the existing destruction, we must renew the limitations upon our celebrations. We who see the remnants of the destroyed Temple before out eyes with only the Western Wall remaining, are required to show more consideration, more seriousness."

He now turned to his practical proposal. "Let us summon the entire Jerusalem community to the *Kothel* and try by prayer to assuage the great wrath being visited upon us from heaven. Let us here accept as one man an eternal ban upon us and our children, and their children after them, to the end of time to prohibit all orchestras and musical instruments at each and every wedding taking place in Jerusalem."

The suggestion was accepted unanimously. The *Gaon* of Kalish finished his message, and Rav Shmuel Salant, who was the official rabbi of the city, rose to give thanks to *Hashem* for having directed His Jerusalem flock in the right direction, and to the Kalisher Rabbi for being the heavenly messenger for the salvation of the community. He also added to the main suggestion that it would be particularly fitting to assemble all the Jews of Jerusalem at midnight, the time commonly accepted as the favorable hour for the acceptance of prayers, the *eith ratzon*. This proposal was also accepted unanimously by the gathering.

A town crier left the *beith din* to make the rounds of the city and announce the proposed assembly by the *Kothel*. On the Friday night of that week, at midnight, men, women and children streamed to the Western Wall to pour out their prayers

74

and to listen to the messages of their leaders.

Rivers of tears were poured out at the *Kothel* square. Giants of Torah, leaders of Jerusalem Jewry, men who had left positions of honor in the Diaspora, went up one after the other to arouse the people to repentance, each confessing his lack of substantial reproof for the Jews of Jerusalem who fulfilled the Torah through deprivation and self-sacrifice. Yet, they added, who knows how exacting *Hashem* is with His righteous followers? Who knows how much is being demanded of the pure dwellers of Jerusalem?

Precedents from the Sages for the Ban

The procession of speakers was rounded out by Rav Yaakov Leib Levi, who had not yet completely recovered from the death of his older brother, Rav Nachum of Shadik. In a keen voice he reviewed a story of the *Gemara* word for word.

"If a person has been bitten by a snake, he should bring a pregnant white donkey, extract its offspring and place of its flesh upon the bite. However, this will help him only if the animal is unblemished. A guard in the city of Pumpaditha was once bitten by a snake. There were thirteen pregnant donkeys which were all fetched and their offspring removed. All of them were found to be blemished. Meanwhile he learned of yet another white donkey on the other side of the city, but before it was fetched, a lion came and ravaged it. Abaye then said, 'Perhaps a *"nachash"*, whose numerical value is *"cherem"*, prohibition, has been violated, in which case there is no remedy.' 'You are correct, *rebbe*,' they said to him, 'for when Rav died Rabbi Yitzchak bar Bisana decreed not to bring *hadassim* leaves or cedar trees, which were used as percussion instruments, to weddings. This man went and brought such instruments to a wedding and was subsequently bitten by the *nachash* and died.'

"We are living through difficult times," the head of the *beith din* wept. "Torah scrolls are burning; *tzaddikim* and worthy men are leaving us one after the other. The settlement is steadily decreasing, who knows to what degree. Within the span of one year three bright stars have fallen from heaven to earth; the souls of three giants of Torah and purity left us in the prime of their years. Is this not the time to renew the ban mentioned by our Sages following the death of a great man? Is this not the time for each one of us to decrease his personal *simcha* in some measure, particularly at its height when a Jew is fortunate to lead his child to the *chuppa*?"

The rabbi's voice trembled but continued, "In a decree promulgated by the *batey din* and all the scholars of the Holy City, and with the approval of the all the *Mekubalim* of the Beith El *yeshiva*, we hereby place a stringent prohibition against any man or woman playing a musical instrument at a wedding. This prohibition applies to the *chathan*, the *kalla* and the in-laws, and is incumbent upon the players and all the guests. Let no succeeding *beith din* ever have any power to nullify this stringent prohibition for any reason whatsoever until we are worthy of receiving our *Mashiach*."

He now turned to the chief rabbi of the Sefardim, one of the central *Mekubalim* of Beith El, the great Rav Chaim David Chazan, son of the famous author of *Chikrei Lev*, to conclude this momentous assembly with the recital of some *Tehillim*. The head of the Sefardic community acquiesced to the request of his Ashkenazi counterpart and began with the *Shir Hama'aloth*.

The entire congregation echoed him, verse for verse.

The prayers ended at dawn. Most of the menfolk remained for an early *vathikin minyan* while the women returned home bearing their children on their arms, nursing the hope that salvation had come.

And indeed, within several days the Jews of Jerusalem were convinced that their hopes were not disappointed. The epidemic abated. Life slowly returned to its normal pace; the prohibition was accepted in all its stringency and the Jews of Jerusalem quickly forgot what they had lived through.

The Lovers of Zion Movement

Rav Meir Auerbach himself was the only person not calmed by the abated plague. For several weeks he had been trying to get the leaders abroad to concur with the Jerusalem prohibition against musical instruments, his reasoning being that perhaps future immigrants to the Holy Land might not properly appreciate the strictness of the ban and would slight it.

But Rav Meir had another thought in mind. Not in vain did he labor to win the concurrence of the Diaspora leaders for the Jerusalem ban.

The movement of *Chovevei Zion* was just beginning to be active in Eretz Yisrael, its aim being to gather the various Jewish communities abroad for a mass immigration to Eretz Yisrael. At first this movement was headed by several Torah leaders including Rav Zvi Hirsh Kalisher, Rabbi of Teheran, Iran. But the majority of Torah leaders soon perceived a spiritual danger in this plan of massive immigration before G-d so willed it—a foresight that was later proven correct when the Lovers of Zion movement was joined by desecrators of the Torah. They therefore opposed the movement violently.

Leading the opposition were those closest to the situation, the Jerusalem leaders, headed by the famed *halachic* researcher of laws pertaining to Eretz Yisrael, Rav Yosef Schwartz, author of *Tvuoth Ha'aretz*, who had labored energetically for the renewed settlement. When his death followed the demise of three of the city's leaders, all as a result of the plague, Rav Hirsh publicized the view that the epidemic and the resulting deaths were a heavenly retribution for the opposition to the *Chovevei Zion* movement.

Rav Meir Auerbach who had conducted a written campaign against the movement in Jerusalem's first periodical, feared that people might take Rav Hirsh's slander to heart. When he now learned the true reason for the plague, he hurried to convey his findings to the Jewish leadership abroad.

In that same year, Jews abroad were deeply shaken by the deaths of their guiding lights, the great *chassidic rebbe*, author of *Chidushei Harim*, who died on the 23d of Adar, 5626 (1866), and the Tzemach Tzeddek, Rav Menachem Mendel of Lubavitch in Russia. The Chidushei Harim was succeeded by Rav Avraham of Checheno, the son of a simple Jew suspected of being one of the *lamed vov tzaddikim* of his generation. At first, people paid no particular attention to the man serving in the small village since he shied away from recognition, but upon the death of the Chidushei Harim people from all over Poland began thronging to him. Within a short time he became the unofficial leader of all Polish Jewry.

Rav Avraham was a violent opponent of the *Chovevei Zion* movement. Rav Meir saw it as his duty to inform Rav Avraham of his Divine revelation and of the subsequent prohibition against musical instruments which Jerusalem Jewry had accepted upon itself.

Rav Avraham, who knew Rav Meir from the time of his rabbinate in Kalish, worded his reply in one sentence:

"You were not named Meir in vain for you have had the privilege of enlightening the eyes of Jewry in the darkness of the *galuth*."

The successor of the Tzemach Tzeddek, also known later for his virulent opposition to the *Chovevei Zion* movement, received the information from Jerusalem and rushed to send his own reply:

"I have a tradition from the Tzemach Tzeddek that the man who will succeed in disclosing the reason behind the suffering of the past year and the demise of the *tzaddikim* in Jerusalem and abroad is the *gadol hador*, the leader of the generation! Fortunate are you, Rav Meir, for having achieved this."

Other leaders abroad also replied in the same vein. From Lithuania, Rav David Friedman of Karlin and Rav Yitzchak Elchanan of Kovna; from Galicia, Rav Shimon Sofer of Cracow and from Germany, the great Rav Yaakov Ettlinger, author of *Aroch Laner*. But the letter from Rav Eliyahu Gutmacher of Greiditz, the rabbi before whose holiness all the other leaders trembled, made the greatest impression of all.

Rav Eliyahu had first numbered among the supporters of Rav Hirsh Kalisher, but he began retracting his position when the latter began to include in his program several communal figures who were not stringent in their *mitzva* observance. When Rav Eliyahu learned the reason behind the Jerusalem ban on musical instruments, he rejected Rav Hirsh completely, sending a letter to Rav Meir Auerbach in which he thanked him for pointing out the truth. He informed the Jerusalem rabbi that

79

he was joining him in his ban on music at weddings in the Old City.

A Break in the Wall of the Prohibition

From that time on, the prohibition on musicians was upheld in the Old City and accepted by all the ages of Jewry. Even new immigrants from the Diaspora kept it reverently. But as with every new amendment, this one was also challenged with occasional attempts at violation.

The first violation took place in 5633 (1873), a year that saw a large influx of immigrants to Jerusalem, among them many outstanding Torah personalities. Many of them were surprised at the ban. Our Sages had, after all, ruled that "everyone who gladdens the *chathan* and *kalla* merits the five voices in the world-to-come." Throughout the generations, even among the most impoverished of paupers, no one had ever dreamed of holding a wedding without musicians. How was it that here, in Jerusalem of all places, a ban and prohibition should be proclaimed against it? One of the immigrants, a man who had served in a prestigious rabbinical position abroad, was about to marry off a daughter. Prior to the event he prepared a long written dissertation in which he attempted to convince the Rabbi of Kalish to permit him to bring musicians, arguing that he had already set a date for the event while abroad. This noted man's opposition to the ban aroused a great controversy in Jerusalem circles, but the Rabbi of Kalish refused to even discuss the matter. Instead he sent for the man and told him the history of the ban in privacy. The rabbi retracted his opposition.

Not so his wife. Being herself the descendant of a noted

family, she stubbornly held on. When she was unable to find musicians who dared break the ban, she hired two Armenian musicians. The Rabbi of Kalish sent her a warning, but she remained adamant in her refusal. On the morning following the wedding a shock wave rippled through the city—the woman had disappeared. All searches proved futile.

The ban on musical instruments was strengthened once more, this time, however, by this most tragic incident.

The Brisker Rav Joins the Prohibition

The Lion of Babylon, Rav Yehoshua Leib Diskin of Brisk, arrived to settle in Jerusalem in the year 5637 (1877). The two monarchs of Torah, the *Gaon* of Kalish and the *Gaon* of Brisk did not have much opportunity to share one crown, but during the several months before the former passed away (on the 25th of Iyar, 5638 [1878]) he managed to transmit to the *Gaon* of Brisk the gist of the amendments and prohibitions which the Jerusalem inhabitants had accepted upon themselves, among them the ban on music.

Rav Eliezer Dan Ralbag, the Brisker Rav's personal *shamash*, who was present at the momentous occasion, used to relate that when the *Gaon* of Brisk heard the entire chapter of the ban and the chain of events leading up to it, he fell down heavily in a faint from which he was not easily revived. In his account, Rav Eliezer Dan would add that the special awe the Brisker Rav nurtured for the sanctity of Jerusalem, and the site of the Temple in particular, was a spiritual legacy he inherited from his grandfather, Rav Leibele Chassid of Slonim who had emigrated to Eretz Yisrael in the year 5568 (1808), together with the saintly Rav David Shlomo Eibushitz of Sirka, author of *Levushei Srad* and *Arvei Nachal*. Because of their great awe and fear of the sanctity of Jerusalem, they decided to settle in Safed where Rav Leibele was buried at the young age of thirty-six.

Rav Leibele numbered among the disciples of the *Gaon* of Vilna. He was known by the name of Rav Leibele Rashis, being a descendent of Rashi. He emigrated to Eretz Yisrael because of the curiosity his neighbors exhibited about his personal, hidden habits and customs. Rav Leibele had only one son and one daughter. The son was later known as the great Rav Binyamin Diskin, father of Rav Yehoshua Leib of Brisk, while the daughter Rivka, who emigrated to Eretz Yisrael with her parents, became the mother of the great Rav Eliezer Dan.

Years passed during which there was no threat or break in the ban. In 5682 (1922), when the settlement expanded with increased immigration, one of the rabbis turned to the Rabbi of Jerusalem, Rav Yosef Chayim Sonnenfeld, asking about the origins of the ban. In his letter, Rav Yosef Chayim replied curtly: "As far as I know, the great author of *Imrei Bina* proclaimed the ban and whoever slighted it was severely punished."

The rabbi was not satisfied with this terse reply and demanded more details. Rav Yosef Chayim answered again:

"I have already written that the Imrei Bina issued the prohibition. I heard my master the *Gaon* of Brisk say, 'Surely in Jerusalem it is a worthy practice . . . where the ruins of the *Beith HaMikdash* are before our very eyes.'"

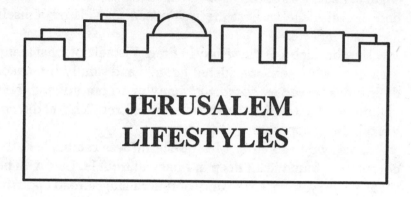

JERUSALEM LIFESTYLES

The Tribulations of Meah Shearim *Meshulachim*

In those times, a *meshulach*, or fund raiser, did not receive his appointment by random selection. Not everyone who presented himself for the post was accepted. A thorough selection was made from the list of candidates before Jerusalem Jews conferred the prestigious post upon their scholarly, exemplary choice who, in addition to his vast Torah knowledge, had to incorporate a full complement of the necessary worthy traits and talents to be able to proudly represent Jerusalem. The *shadar* (*shaliach d'rabbanan*) needed, in addition, to be blessed with the power of persuasion and expression so that he could delineate to Diaspora Jews the duty and great value of Torah support for those dwelling upon the mountain of G-d.

And indeed, throughout the communities abroad, the *shadar* from Eretz Yisrael was accorded great respect. Everyone was eager to hear news of the *yishuv* in the Holy Land, and whoever had the privilege to host the *meshulach* considered himself fortunate indeed.

The chronicles of the *yishuv* in Eretz Yisrael note that many great men who were considered *gaonim* and saintly figures of their times served as *shadarim*, many of whom utilized their visits abroad to publish their works, since Eretz Yisrael did not yet offer that opportunity.

Some two years after Meah Shearim was established, the corporation found itself deep in financial trouble. Left with no recourse, they imposed the duty of fundraising abroad upon the person of Rabbi Yehoshua Chaimsohn.

A great scholar and a leading figure in the area of *kedusha* and communal needs, Rabbi Yehoshua also had access to highly-placed officials in the Turkish government which then ruled the country. Being thoroughly versed in Turkish, he served as interpreter between the authorities and the Jerusalem Jewish community. Later on, he was even appointed Prussian consul to the Middle East. All these factors contributed to his selection as the choice representative of the Meah Shearim community.

The Jerusalem rabbis sent out letters to all the major European cities, asking the communal heads to welcome the Jerusalem representative with due respect and esteem and to extend him a generous helping hand so that the Meah Shearim corporation could extract itself from debt and continue its work of expanding and rebuilding the Holy City.

All the heads of both the Sefardic and Ashkenazi communities signed the *kthav shlichuth*, the official authorization, and Rabbi Yehoshua Chaimsohn set upon his journey.

There was one charlatan in London, a Jew known for his

chicanery, who learned of Rabbi Yehoshua's mission and understood that European Jewry would surely open its purse to this *shaliach* from Jerusalem, both individually and communally. He decided to masquerade as the Jerusalem *shadar* and present himself as Rabbi Yehoshua Chaimsohn.

Through various tricks, he succeeded in forging the signatures of the Jerusalem rabbis and *kolel* heads. Knowing that Rabbi Yehoshua's itinerary placed Poland as his first stop, from where he would travel on to Italy, he preceded him and went directly to Italy.

Italian rabbis had meanwhile received the letters and recommendations sent on ahead by the Jerusalem *rabbanim*, asking them to prepare their emissary's reception. That very week, the impostor *shaliach* arrived, armed with forged credentials. He was accorded a royal reception and flooded with donations and gifts. Wherever he turned, doors were opened wide. People rejoiced at the privilege of receiving this prestigious guest.

His stay was most pleasant; he was in no hurry to return to London. Meanwhile, however, Rabbi Yehoshua the Jerusalemite had finished his work in the other European countries and was making his way towards Italy. His first stop was Livorno, the very city where the impostor *shadar* had been staying for the past two weeks.

Before entering any city, Rabbi Yehoshua would send a special letter on ahead via his personal aide to the rabbi of the city, noting the date of his arrival so that a proper reception might be arranged as befit the delegate of the prestigious Holy City of Jerusalem, which he was representing. This time, too, before entering Livorno, he sent his letter on before him.

The Rabbi of Livorno was shocked when he read the letter. He immediately sent for the first *shaliach* and showed it to him.

The Londoner did not lose his wits, having apparently been prepared for such a confrontation.

"I have no idea what is going on here!" he replied with ironic cool. "Surely some blackguard has been following my trail, thinking that I had not yet visited this city. Actually, I have already heard of this impostor; he has an old reputation. Providence has arranged for a confrontation in Livorno to punish him for his fraud and for having embezzled the money rightfully belonging to the Jerusalem community."

The *rav* swallowed this spiel and put the matter aside, making mental note of it for future use, feeling that something was in the offing.

Rabbi Yehoshua reached Livorno on *Erev Shabbath*; to his stupefaction, no one came out to greet him. This had never happened to him before in all his travels, nor had such a thing ever transpired in the history of other *shlichim* from Jerusalem. His letter had perhaps been mislaid, he conjectured, which explained why the populace was so ignorant of his arrival.

He had no choice but to seek lodgings at one of the city's hostels. On the following morning, he asked one of the servants of the hotel to take him to the central *beith knesseth* where the *rav davened*. When they arrived, the place was already packed from wall to wall. Rabbi Yehoshua asked his companion to kindly approach the rabbi and inform him that the *shaliach* from Jerusalem had arrived. Rabbi Yehoshua imagined that as soon as the rabbi heard of his arrival, he would rise and lead him to the prestigious place at the eastern wall, as befitted the representative of the Holy City. To his great amazement and disappointment, the *shamash* of the *shul* approached him and led him to a place behind the stove, the traditional corner of the commoner folk.

"There must be some terrible mistake," Rabbi Yehoshua thought, repeating his words to the *shamash*, in a firmer tone this time, telling him to inform the *rav* that Rabbi Yehoshua Chaimsohn, the Jerusalem *shaliach*, was present. The *shamash* returned and relayed the message to the *rav*, but the *rav* did not react.

Meanwhile, the pretender was occupying a seat of distinction on the eastern wall, next to the rabbi. Before long, the congregation rose up in arms—they clearly saw the Jerusalem *shadar* sitting in his rightful place while a brazen impostor sought to displace him and claim the honor for himself! How could a Jew stoop so low? Who dared betray the public trust by conniving with money set aside for the Jews of Jerusalem? The congregation seethed. They swarmed around Rabbi Yehoshua, warning him that if he did not confess his sin publicly, he would be dragged in chains to the jailhouse right after *Shabbath*. Within minutes, several *mithpallilim* had raised their hands against him, warning the "pretender" that his shame had been exposed only because the true *shaliach* from Jerusalem had preceded him in visiting this city.

Rabbi Yehoshua's spirits did not fail. He paid no attention to all the curses and imprecations heaped upon him, nor even to the hands physically raised against him. The tragedy of errors began to dawn on him. Some scoundrel had been imposing upon the city's hospitality for two weeks, in his name. Rabbi Yehoshua understood that he must act immediately before the charlatan managed to escape after *Shabbath*. Evading his attackers, he jumped upon a bench and began speaking in a loud voice.

"Dear rabbis and friends," he announced. "I am the true *shaliach* from Jerusalem. If anyone in this synagogue is appearing in my name, claiming that he represents the rabbis of

Jerusalem, then he is the real cheater and impostor!"

Rabbi Yehoshua's venerable appearance and his forceful words had a great impact upon his attackers. Several of them went up to the *rav* to consult in whispers. Here, indeed, was a riddle. By all appearances, the newcomer to the title seemed to be telling the truth. He seemed to them the more respectable, distinguished person. The truth must be carefully investigated. The rabbi whispered back that he had suspected something amiss when the first *shaliach* had appeared but had been circumspect about challenging him. Meanwhile, he called for everyone to retain his present place and come to order.

The rabbi then instructed that the first *shaliach* be honored with the coveted *shlishi aliya* to the Torah, while the claimant, the second *shaliach*, be given *shvi'i*.

Rabbi Yehoshua of Jerusalem ascended the *bima* to the baleful stare of dozens of eyes. A hum of whispering was audible.

"It is hard to believe such terrible things of a Jew like that!" one could hear Reb Menashe the bathhouse attendant whisper.

"Did you note his distinguished look, his angelic form?" Reb Chaim the barber was heard to counter. "I can judge people by their appearance through certain signs my grandfather transmitted to me. I would not want to say for sure, but who knows if he is not the real *meshulach*?"

"You still have doubts in the matter? When I heard his sweet, inspiring voice reciting the blessing over the Torah and the way it contrasted with our first *shaliach*'s voice, which I had heard several times before, *lehavdil*, I decided that the first one is the impostor and the second one, the *shaliach* from Jerusalem."

This last voice could also be heard in the *beith knesseth*

88

auditorium, but since the *gabbai* kept on pounding the table for silence, its owner could not be identified.

The reader finished the *parsha*, and Rabbi Yehoshua recited the concluding blessing over the Torah, under the careful scrutiny of the congregation. Suddenly, he burst into bitter tears.

"*Ribono Shel Olam*," he announced. "You are the only one here Who knows the truth. For the sake of Jerusalem's honor, for the sake of Jerusalem scholars and paupers, show Your might and glory. Let them not find cause to be ashamed of their representative, Your humble servant, to whom they raise their eyes in expectation and hope."

Silence reigned in the large hall. Eyes were fixed upon the *bima*. The original impostor began trembling violently, but still managed to cry out, "Rabbi Yehoshua, I am the scoundrel and you the *tzaddik*," before he fainted. The rush of people now changed direction as help was extended to the fallen man.

The unconscious man was removed to the women's gallery. The congregation was stunned, thunderstruck. Some people recovered enough to approach Rabbi Yehoshua and beg his forgiveness.

The *rav*, much moved by the episode, also approached the Jerusalem *shaliach* to seek his forgiveness and to invite him to the *Shabbath* meal in his home. The *davening* over, the entire congregation poured out of the synagogue to escort Rabbi Yehoshua to his new lodgings at the rabbi's home, with song and dance and praise to *Hashem* for His having shown them His wonders, in the merit of Jerusalem Jewry.

Rabbi Yehoshua won acclaim in all the neighboring countries. Wherever he went, he was revered as a G-dly man and extended a doubly generous hand. And, indeed, this trip proved to be most successful in easing the financial pressures of

Jerusalem Jewry and of the Meah Shearim corporation in particular.

His bushel of troubles was not yet full, however, as became apparent upon his return voyage to Jerusalem.

The huge sum of money which Rabbi Yehoshua carried, he hid under his head each night while his attendant, Reb Avraham Leib stood guard. The ship they traveled upon was Greek, as were most of the sailors. Sensing the treasure that the two Jews were concealing, the crew plotted to kill the two men and divide the booty amongst themselves.

Reb Avraham Leib, whose room adjoined the one in which the vile deed was being hatched, overheard snatches of the murderers' conversation and learned of the scheme. Frightened and agitated, he related to Rabbi Yehoshua what he had over-heard. Rabbi Yehoshua reassured him, however, saying that he was confident that *Hashem*, Who had watched over them throughout their journey and had wrought miracles all along, would certainly guard them now so that no harm would befall them.

The murderers attempted to carry out their vile deed that very night, when all the passengers were deep in slumber. One of them opened Rabbi Yehoshua's door quietly, inserted his hand into his belt and withdrew a glittering, razor-sharp knife. He was just about to plunge the blade into Rabbi Yehoshua's heart, when suddenly his hand froze, paralyzed, and the knife clattered to the ground. Rabbi Yehoshua awakened. The Greek was seized by excruciating pain; his screams drew a crowd of passengers who were confronted by the frightening scene. Rabbi Yehoshua lying on his bed, the long, shining knife lying on the floor and beside it one of the ship's sailors, screaming from the pain of his suddenly paralyzed hand.

The rest of the plotters also rushed to the scene. Terrified by Rabbi Yehoshua's power, they fell upon their knees before him, begging forgiveness for their evil intentions and pleading that he heal their stricken comrade. Rabbi Yehoshua promised to pray for the man, and later that very day, the sailor regained the use of his hand. *Hashem's* Name had been glorified.

From then on, the gentiles aboard ship regarded the two Jewish passengers with awe, fulfilling their every need most servilely, until the latter debarked in Jaffa.

From the time Rabbi Yehoshua returned, the Meah Shearim community was able to breathe freely. For the rest of his life, Rabbi Yehoshua commemorated that day aboard ship when he had been saved by a miracle, as a day of feasting, rejoicing and thanksgiving to G-d. This practice was perpetuated later by his descendants.